Geor
and th

By the same author

George H. Ghastly
George H. Ghastly to the Rescue

George H. Ghastly
and the
Little Horror

Ritchie Perry

Illustrated by Chris Winn

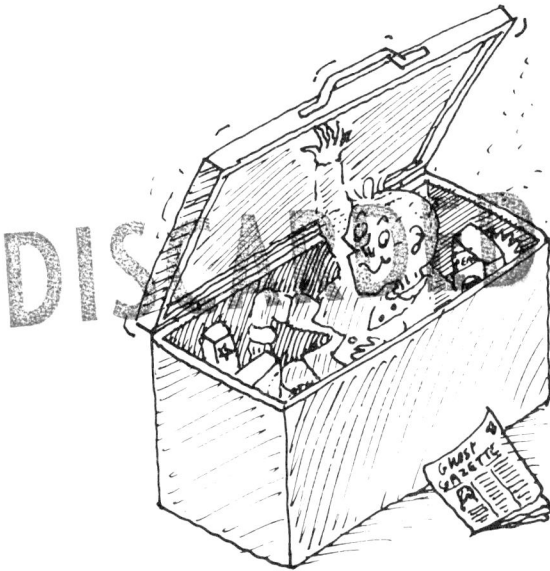

Hutchinson
London Melbourne Sydney Auckland Johannesburg

Hutchinson Children's Books Ltd

An imprint of the Hutchinson Publishing Group

17–21 Conway Street, London W1P 6JD

Hutchinson Publishing Group (Australia) Pty Ltd
16–22 Church Street, Hawthorn, Melbourne, Victoria 3122,
Australia

Hutchinson Group (NZ) Ltd
32–34 View Road, PO Box 40-086, Glenfield, Auckland 10

Hutchinson Group (SA) Pty Ltd
PO Box 337, Bergvlei 2012, South Africa

First published 1985
© Ritchie Perry 1985
Illustrations © Chris Winn 1985
Set in Baskerville by BookEns, Saffron Walden, Essex

Printed and bound in Great Britain by Anchor Brendon Ltd,
Tiptree, Essex

British Library cataloguing in Publication Data

Perry, Ritchie
  George H. Ghastly and the little horror.
  I. Title
  823'.914[J]   PZ7

ISBN 0 09 162460 6

One

Fenella Fang had finally finished packing her coffin. Everything she would need was neatly stored and there was plenty of room for her to climb in as well. Fenella stepped back and allowed herself a small smile of satisfaction. It was this smile, revealing her teeth to perfection, which had charmed the judges at the Miss Vampire of the Year competition and won her the first prize of a trip to Transylvania. Of course, no humans would have been at all charmed by her smile. They would have been scared stiff but human beings never had understood vampires. Fond as she was of him, Fenella knew that this was mainly Uncle Dracula's fault. He was the one who had done most to give vampires a bad name. People didn't realize that since the discovery of HBS*, vampires left humans well alone. At least, they did unless they were really hungry.

*HBS – Human Blood Substitute

1

With the packing completed, there was only one thing left for Fenella to do. After a quick check to make sure that she had left her crypt neat and tidy, she went outside and started up the hill towards Mr Merryfellow's house. Although she could have flown, it wasn't very far and Fenella preferred to walk. In any case, George had never liked her in her bat form. He said she looked like a kite with teeth.

When she arrived at the house, Fenella waited outside. No vampire could enter a human house without an invitation. This was why George usually came to visit her in the crypt.

'George,' she called out softly. 'I'm here.'

No human ear could have heard her voice but to a ghost like George it should have been clearly audible. However, there was no answer.

'George,' she called again. 'It's Fenella. Where are you?'

George was up in the attic. Like most ghosts, there was nothing he enjoyed more than dressing up and pretending to be a human. As Fenella was going to be away for a month, he had wanted to wear something really special to mark the occasion and he had been hunting through the trunks full of Mr Merryfellow's old clothes. He had been putting the final touches to his appearance when Fenella first called. On his head he had a top hat and a pair of goggles which drivers had worn when cars were first invented. To cover his body he was wearing a swimming costume, one of the old-fashioned kind which came down to his elbows and knees. For footwear he had some rugby boots which dated back to Mr Merryfellow's college days.

When Fenella called the second time, George made a final adjustment to the hat which kept slipping down over his eyes, and hurried off to greet her.

'How do I look?' he asked as soon as they were inside.

'Magnificent,' Fenella told him. 'Absolutely superb.'

To tell the truth, she thought George looked rather silly. However, she liked him far too much to risk hurting his feelings.

'That's what I thought.' George always liked compliments. 'You look very nice too, Fenella. Is that a new shroud you're wearing?'

'It's just a little something I ran up myself,' Fenella said modestly. 'I needed something new for the trip.'

As she had a hearse to catch, Fenella couldn't stay very long. Although the bat's blood daiquiris and toadstool sandwiches which George had prepared were very good, neither of them was very cheerful.

'I'm going to miss you, Fenella,' George said mournfully for the third time.

'I'll miss you too, Horrible.' Horrible was

George's middle name. Only his mother and Fenella ever used it. 'But it's only for a month.'

'A month can seem an awful long time when you're on your own.'

'You won't be on your own, though. Mr Merryfellow will still be here to keep you company.'

'I know, but he goes to sleep every night. Just like you sleep during the day.'

Ghosts didn't sleep at all. In fact, George wasn't sure what sleep really was. He had tried closing his eyes once or twice to find out but all that happened was that he couldn't see where he was going.

'What's it like, Horrible?' Fenella asked suddenly. 'Having a human as a friend?'

'He's just like you or me, except that he's alive. We get on very well together.'

'Don't you ever want to haunt any more?'

'Not really.' This was a subject which rather embarrassed George. 'I'm used to the idea that human beings think I'm funny.'

For once George wasn't being completely honest. Deep down he would still have liked to be a proper ghost who could frighten human beings without using tricks. In fact, when he was on his own at night, George often spent hours in front of a mirror practising hideous faces and blood-curdling screams. It wasn't any good, though. If he tried them out on his friend, Mr Merryfellow

simply laughed and said what a comical little
fellow he was.

'Do you know something, Horrible? You're
always talking about this Mr Merryfellow of yours
but I've never actually seen him.'

'Haven't you?'

George was surprised.

'No, no once.'

'That's easy to put right. You can take a look at
him now if you have the time and you're careful
not to disturb him.'

Fenella promised and George showed her to
Mr Merryfellow's bedroom. While she went
inside, George drifted up to the attic to remove his
borrowed clothes. He was still there a few minutes
later when Mr Merryfellow started screaming.

It wasn't really Fenella's fault and to begin with
everything was all right. As George had said, Mr
Merryfellow was fast asleep in bed, snoring
happily. Without a sound, Fenella had moved
from the door to stand beside the bed. She was
curious and, in a way, she rather envied George.
Fenella had often thought how much easier death
would be if she didn't have to hide from human
beings. There would be no more daymares about
some human creeping up to her coffin with a
hammer and stake while she was asleep. People
wouldn't be nearly so frightened of vampires if

they realized how frightened vampires were of them.

Even when she was standing close to the bed, Fenella couldn't see Mr Merryfellow very well. This wasn't simply because it was dark in the bedroom. What with the bedclothes and Mr Merryfellow's nightcap, there was very little of him to see apart from his nose. Although it was quite a nice nose, Fenella had been hoping to see a bit more of George's friend.

For a moment Fenella hesitated. Then, her mind made up, she bent and pulled back the bedclothes from Mr Merryfellow's face, moving them very gently so as not to disturb him. She could see at once why George liked him so much. Mr Merryfellow had a friendly face, the kind of face it would be very difficult not to like. Even while he was asleep, there appeared to be a smile on his lips. It made Fenella smile fondly as well. Unfortunately, this was the exact moment Mr Merryfellow chose to open his eyes.

Mr Merryfellow was quite a brave man. Apart from spiders and daddy-long-legs, he didn't frighten easily but he had never had a vampire come visiting in the middle of the night before. As soon as he saw Fenella, he knew exactly what she was about to do. The way her long teeth gleamed as she leaned over him left him in no doubt about this at all.

'Hhheeelllppp,' he screamed at the top of his

voice. 'It's a hideous, blood-sucking vampire. It's come to gobble me up as a late-night snack.'

Then he ducked down under the blankets where the rest of his screams were muffled. Poor Fenella was aghast at what had happened. She hadn't intended to frighten him. She wanted to explain to Mr Merryfellow that she didn't mean him any harm. This was why she started to pull the blankets back.

'It's all right—,' she began.

There was no chance to finish because Mr Merryfellow wasn't listening to her. All he knew was that the vampire seemed to be coming after him.

'HHHEEELLLPPP,' he shrieked even louder than before. 'Save me, somebody. There's a great, big, horrible vampire climbing into bed with me.'

Fenella dropped the covers in dismay and fled from the room. In the corridor outside, she met George who had rushed down from the attic as soon as he heard the commotion. Although he had removed some of the borrowed clothes, he was still wearing the top hat and the swimming costume.

'Goodness gracious, Horrible,' Fenella said, sounding as flustered as she felt. 'I hadn't realized it was this late. I really must rush before the hearse leaves without me. Goodbye.'

'But, Fenella . . . .'

George discovered that he was talking to her retreating back and he couldn't possibly abandon Mr Merryfellow to chase after her.

When he went into the bedroom, he found that his friend was still huddled under the covers, a large, quaking lump in the middle of the bed. Even after George had identified himself, Mr Merryfellow refused to come out immediately.

'It's a trick,' he declared. 'I know who you are. You're not George. You're a vampire and you want me for your supper.'

It was several minutes before George could persuade him to emerge from hiding. Mr Merryfellow was still shaking like a badly set jelly.

'It was a vampire,' he kept repeating. 'A great, slavering beast with long fangs.'

'There wasn't a vampire in the bedroom when I came in.' George was being absolutely truthful. He also thought Mr Merryfellow was being most unkind about Fenella's appearance. 'The room was quite empty.'

'You must have scared it away then. Are you sure you haven't had any of your family over to visit?'

Mr Merryfellow would never forget the night he had met George's father. Or, to be more accurate, the night he had met Mr Ghastly's head. This had frightened him almost as much as Fenella had.

'I'm positive,' George told him. 'Couldn't you have been dreaming?'

By this time Mr Merryfellow wasn't really sure of anything. If you lived in a house with a ghost who floated around wearing a top hat and a bathing costume in the middle of the night, there was no telling what might happen. Now Mr Merryfellow thought about it, it could have been a dream as George had suggested, although it had seemed frighteningly real at the time. Just to be on the safe side, though, Mr Merryfellow left the light on in his bedroom when George eventually left him and it was a long time before he went back to sleep. As for George, he returned to the attic to remove the rest of his costume, very relieved to have escaped from an awkward situation. He wasn't to know that in the very near future he would find himself in a far worse situation. Far, far worse.

Two

The Brat was what everybody called Bertrand Buckle when they were being nice about him. When they weren't being nice, the names they called him were far less complimentary. Early the morning following Mr Merryfellow's adventure with Fenella, nobody was being at all nice about Bertrand. He was in trouble which was where he normally was: it was a very unusual day when he didn't get into some mischief or other. Even when he had had to stay in bed with measles, he had nearly burst the doctor's eardrums by shouting into his stethoscope.

Bertrand was in Mr Whackem's office at St Joseph's School, standing in front of the headmaster's desk. One glance at him was all that was necessary to tell what kind of a boy he was. He couldn't have looked any scruffier if he had spent the past week walking backwards and forwards through haystacks, stopping every now and then to roll in a large patch of mud. Small twigs and pieces of grass stuck out of his unkempt hair. His face and hands didn't look as though they had ever heard of soap and water. One pocket of his blazer was completely ripped off and the other bulged with all the useful objects Bertrand carried around with him – conkers, stink bombs, itching powder and his pet mouse, Squeak. His trousers were soaked to the knees and covered with weed – the result of an attempt to jump across the school fishpond which had failed. His shoes, also soaked, had no laces in them because he had used them to tie Muriel Meek to her peg in the cloakroom. And this was how Bertrand looked at half-past nine in the morning. By the end of the day he was really untidy.

Mr and Mrs Buckle were also in the headmaster's office, sitting on seats at the side of the room. They had been asked to come into school so that Mr Whackem could discuss Bertrand's behaviour with them for the umpteenth time. Mr Buckle was a thin, tired looking man with a balding head and a nervous twitch in his right cheek. Mrs Buckle was plumper but appeared to be equally tired. Her nervous twitch was beneath her left eye. Everybody who had to spend much time in Bertrand's company looked tired and had a nervous twitch.

'It simply can't go like this,' Mr Whackem said severely.

Mr Buckle sighed wearily. This was something he had been through on many occasions and at several different schools.

'What's the little dev— I mean Bertrand done now?' he asked.

'I'm afraid I don't have the time to go through the whole of this week's list, not unless you want to stay to lunch.' Mr Whackem was very good at sarcasm. 'I'll just select one or two of the highlights. Bertrand, you can wait outside until I send for you.'

'Yes, sir,' Bertrand mumbled.

'Silly old sausage,' he added under his breath as he turned away.

Bertrand shambled out into the secretary's office, slamming the door behind him. Once there, he hunted for somewhere to put the stale piece of chewing-gum he had in his mouth. Later it would take three days before the secretary could get her typewriter working properly again.

'Well now,' Mr Whackem said to Bertrand's parents. 'Let's see what the Br— young Bertrand has been up to recently.'

The headmaster had a large piece of paper on the desk in front of him which was covered with writing.

'Oh, yes. For a start Bertrand removed the handle on the door of the staff toilet so that nobody could go in or out. Unfortunately, Miss Faucet happened to be in the toilet when the incident occurred. It was two hours before she was discovered and another hour before the caretaker could release her. The situation wasn't improved by Bertrand standing outside the toilet window and chanting "Oh dear, what can the matter be? Old Flossie Faucet is locked in the lavatory". By the time the poor woman was set free she was quite hysterical. I had to send her home for the rest of the day so she could calm down.'

'Oh dear,' Mrs Buckle said faintly.

'Oh dear indeed.' Mr Whackem checked further down the long list. 'As if this wasn't bad enough, Bertrand smeared grease on the balance beam in the hall. When Mr Whalebelly stood on it in PE, he slipped straight off again and landed most painfully on his head. We had to take him to hospital to have his nose X-rayed and it won't be out of bandages until the end of next week.'

'Oh dear, oh dear.'

Mrs Buckle's voice was fainter then ever. Her husband had buried his face in his hands.

'There's more yet,' Mr Whackem continued grimly. 'Yesterday the Br— Bertrand nearly scalped the Belcher twins. He tied their pigtails together, then dropped spiders down the backs of their dresses. Unfortunately, they tried to run off in opposite directions. The good news is that the doctor says their hair should grow back again.'

'Oh dear, oh dear, oh dear.'

Now Mrs Buckle was wringing her hands.

'As I said before, things simply can't continue like this.'

'But he does seem to be getting better.' There was a note of desperation in Mr Buckle's voice. 'I mean, Bertrand has had much worse weeks.'

'Today is Wednesday,' Mr Whackem pointed out. 'The week has only just begun.'

'Oh dear, oh dear, oh dear, oh dear. Whatever are we going to do?'

'That, Mrs Buckle, is a very good question indeed.' Mr Whackem settled back in his chair and clasped his hands across his substantial stomach. 'Has it occurred to either of you that a change of air might do the Br— Bertrand good? It would certainly do all the staff and pupils here at St Joseph's a lot of good.'

'And us,' Mr Buckle agreed. 'The trouble is, where on earth can we send him? I mean, nobody in their right minds would want to have Bertrand staying with them.'

'How about his grandparents?' Mr Whackem suggested hopefully.

Mr Buckle was shaking his head vigorously before the headmaster had finished speaking.

'My father won't have Bertrand in the house,' he explained. 'The last time we went to visit, Bertrand tied some roller skates on his Grandad's feet while he was asleep in a deckchair. When he woke and tried to stand up he rolled straight into the fishpond. Dad might have drowned if I hadn't been there to help.'

'My mum doesn't like Bertrand either,' Mrs

Buckle said. 'Not since he plugged her hearing aid into his ghetto blaster. The poor old dear didn't stop shaking for a week.'

'I see.' Mr Whackem was disappointed. He would have expelled the child but Bertrand had already been kicked out of every other school in the area. There was nowhere else to send him. Given a choice, Mr Whackem would have packed Bertrand off to the RSPCA. They were used to little animals there. 'Isn't there anybody at all?'

For a few seconds there was silence in the office. Then Mrs Buckle's face suddenly brightened.

'There's always Matthew,' she said.

'Matthew?' Mr Whackem echoed hopefully.

'Matthew Merryfellow, my brother. He lives up north and he hasn't seen our Bertrand since he was a baby. We could always send him there. I'll write a letter today.'

Suddenly there were smiles on everybody's faces. They were so relieved that none of them spared a thought for what Mr Merryfellow was about to suffer. As they didn't even know that George existed, they couldn't possible spare a thought for him. Or realize that he would suffer most of all.

Three

Mr Merryfellow was absolutely delighted to receive the letter from his only sister. He was even more pleased to discover that his nephew Bertrand was coming to stay with him. As he explained to George, it was almost nine years since he had seen any of his sister's family.

'Why?' George asked. 'If you're so fond of each other, why haven't you kept in touch?'

Ghost families were very close. Although George was as far from his parents as Mr Merryfellow was from his sister, he was always visiting them. He couldn't imagine going nine long years without seeing any of his relatives.

'Now I come to think of it, I don't really know.' Mr Merryfellow scratched his head in perplexity. 'It's almost as though we got out of the habit. Muriel and I always used to see a lot of each other. Even when she and Alfred moved down to London we visited regularly. Then it all seemed to stop. Every time we arranged to see each other, something would go wrong. Of course, Muriel and Alfred have been ill a lot these past few years. It's strange really. They always used to be so healthy. It must be the London air.'

'What about your nephew?' George was becoming excited himself. 'What's Bertrand like?'

'I haven't seen him since he was a toddler but he was the loveliest child you can imagine. Like a little angel he was. Why, he was so well behaved that butter wouldn't have melted in his mouth. You'll like him a lot, George.'

'Will I be able to play with him?'

'I don't know about that.' Mr Merryfellow scratched his head again. 'It might be best if he didn't know about you. People wouldn't understand if they discovered that I had a ghost for a friend.'

This was something George could appreciate easily enough. There was an awful lot of ghosts who couldn't understand how George could possibly be friendly with a human being. All the same, George wasn't entirely happy with the arrangement.

'If I have to keep hidden from Bertrand, I won't be able to spend much time with you.'

'We'll work something out.' Mr Merryfellow was still too excited to share his friend's concern. 'Besides, Bertrand will have to go to the village school while he's here – the holidays don't begin for another fortnight. And boys his age tire easily so he'll be going to bed early ... you'll see. Having him here won't interfere with us very much. All you have to do is make sure Bertrand doesn't learn about you. That shouldn't be difficult.'

This was sufficient to cheer George up. The trouble was that Mr Merryfellow had no idea that the angelic little toddler he remembered had grown up into a monster. Mr and Mrs Buckle had long since learned that it was virtually impossible to keep anything secret from Bertrand for long.

It took Bertrand almost forty-eight hours to discover that his uncle had a ghost in the house with him. If he hadn't been so tired from the train journey, he would probably have found out earlier.

First there had been the excitement of driving the luggage trolley around King's Cross station, whizzing in and out of the passengers until the station master had caught up with him. Then there had been the communication cord on the train itself. Bertrand had only had the opportunity to test it once but it had seemed to work all right. In fact, he had been most impressed. The train had stopped so suddenly when he pulled the cord that most of the other passengers had ended up on the floor. There was one man from the restaurant car with tomato soup and spaghetti all over him who had seemed quite angry so

Bertrand was very glad nobody knew he was responsible.

What with one thing and another, it had been early evening before Bertrand had reached Gigglesworth station where Uncle Matthew was waiting for him. There was only time for a quick meal before he went to bed and he was asleep almost as soon as his head touched the pillow.

The next day had been a busy one as well. Uncle Matthew had spent most of it showing Bertrand around the village and the surrounding district. Bertrand had thoroughly enjoyed himself and, for once in his life, he had been as good as gold. Even the lady who had fainted in the tea shop hadn't really been his fault. He hadn't known that Squeak would try to crawl up her skirt when he was let out for a walk.

There was only one part of the day which Bertrand hadn't enjoyed. He hadn't realized that he would have to go to school while he was staying with his uncle. He had thought it would be a glorious holiday spent climbing trees and damming streams and burrowing into haystacks. Boring old school hadn't played any part in his plans, and now, having met the local headmaster, he was even more determined it wouldn't. Mr Whackem was bad enough but Bertrand only had to take one look at Mr Beak to know that the two of them wouldn't hit it off together. Or, at least, if they did, Bertrand had a pretty fair idea of who

21

would be doing all the hitting. Mr Beak didn't look like the kind of man who would put up with any nonsense.

That night, after he had gone to bed, Bertrand considered the problem. He definitely didn't want to go to school the following morning. He wanted to play at cowboys with the herd of cattle in the field behind Mr Merryfellow's house.

'I know what I need,' Bertrand said to himself in the darkness. 'I need to be sick.'

It was a good idea. In fact, it was an excellent one. However, it needed working on.

'Not sick sick,' he added after a moment. 'I need to be too sick to go to school but not too sick to stop me enjoying myself.'

This was the point at which Bertrand stuck. It would be easy enough to make himself ill. All he had to do was eat a bar of soap or something like that – but then he might have to stay in bed. There had to be a better way to do it.

'Flour,' he said suddenly. 'With flour all over your face, Brat, you'll look really pale and poorly. Uncle Matthew will never send you to school then.'

Bertrand had never been one to waste time. Excitedly he pushed back the covers and swung his legs out of bed. Flour would be kept in the kitchen and this was where he was going straight away. He wanted to experiment to find out how much he would have to use.

Very quietly, Bertrand eased open the bedroom door and, just as he had hoped, Uncle Matthew was in the living room watching television. He could clearly hear the sound of whatever programme it was his uncle was watching. It wasn't until he reached the bottom of the stairs that Bertrand realized his mistake. The noise didn't come from the television set. It was the sound of two people talking. Still on tiptoe, Bertrand crept across to the living-room door to investigate.

'I told you he was a nice boy,' Mr Merryfellow was saying.

'He's all right I suppose.'

If George didn't sound as enthusiastic as his friend, this was because he wasn't. To tell the truth, he was a little bit jealous of all the attention Bertrand was receiving.

'He's no trouble at all,' Mr Merryfellow went on. 'It's going to be a real pleasure to have him staying here.'

Outside the door, Bertrand was smirking to himself. It just went to show what he could do when he was on his best behaviour. He bent down to take another peek through the keyhole. Bertrand could see his uncle clearly enough but so far he hadn't managed to catch a glimpse of the visitor.

'It's only a couple of weeks until the end of the

school term,' Mr Merryfellow was in full flow by now. 'Then we can take dear little Bertrand to all kinds of interesting places. Why, we can even take him to the seaside. He'll enjoy that.'

'The seaside?'

This was somewhere George had never been.

'It's where lots of people go for their holidays,' Mr Merryfellow explained. 'You do know what the sea is, don't you?'

'Of course I do. It's lots of water, like a huge river wthout any banks. The thing I don't understand is what all the people do once they're there.'

'Well, the older ones spend a lot of time sitting in their deck chairs on the sand.'

'You do that at home but you always put your deck chair out on the lawn.'

'That's because I'm not at the seaside.'

'I know but there's a big pile of sand in the garden left over from building the new garage. Why don't you put your deck chair on top of that?'

'It wouldn't be the same, George.' Mr Merryfellow had the feeling that he was beginning to get out of his depth. 'In any case, people don't just sit in deck chairs at the seaside. They do lots of different things. They have picnics on the sand as well.'

'What's a picnic?'

George was becoming really interested now.

He was always fascinated by the strange things that human beings did.

'A picnic is when you make sandwiches and things and eat them in the open air. It's great fun.'

'You mean people eat their food on the sand.'

'That's right.'

Mr Merryfellow was beginning to wish that he had never mentioned the seaside. He had forgotten how complicated the simplest things could become when he tried to explain them to George.

'Is that better than eating from a table?'

'No, not exactly. It's just that a picnic makes a pleasant change if the weather is nice.'

'In that case, why don't you put your deck chair on the pile of sand and eat some sandwiches there?'

George was very pleased with this idea. This was obviously why sandwiches were called sandwiches – they should be eaten on sand. For the death of him, he couldn't understand why Mr Merryfellow was holding his head in his hands and groaning.

'There's more to the seaside than sunbathing and picnics,' he said once he had recovered. 'Lots more. You can go swimming as well.'

'What's swimming?' George asked.

Another groan escaped from Mr Merryfellow's

lips. Words which were quite ordinary to a human being didn't mean anything to a ghost.

'Swimming is when you go into the water and splash around and play.'

'Like the games you always play in the bath with your rubber duck and sponge?'

'More or less.'

'So if you wanted Bertrand to enjoy himself, he could have a bath. Then he could sit on the sand heap in the garden and eat some sandwiches.'

This time Mr Merryfellow kept his head in his hands for much longer. There were times when he was very thankful that he was such a patient man.

'You just don't understand, George,' he wailed plaintively.

'I'm sorry, Matthew.' George really was. He didn't like to see his friend upset. 'It's simply that ghosts don't ever go to the seaside.'

The word 'ghost' made Bertrand stand up so fast that he banged his head on the door handle. He had been thinking that the person Uncle Matthew was talking to must be a complete idiot. Fancy not knowing what a picnic was, or swimming either. But things were very different if this George character really was what he said he was. Ghosts couldn't be expected to know anything about the seaside. They would be kept far too busy haunting for that.

So far Bertrand hadn't managed to see George

through the keyhole. No matter how he twisted and turned, he had been unable to catch a glimpse of him. Now Bertrand stopped listening to the conversation and concentrated instead on opening the door as quietly as possible. Fortunately, the handle didn't squeak at all. Centimetre by centimetre, Bertrand pushed it down until the catch slid free. Then he paused because the next step was the dangerous one. He knew Uncle Matthew had his back to the door but he could only guess at where the ghost was. Bertrand was as careful easing the door open as he had been with the handle. He only had to open it a crack before he could peep into the living-room.

In some ways the ghost was a disappointment to him. Bertrand had always thought of ghosts being scary but there was nothing at all frightening about the one with Uncle Matthew. Old Whackem was far more terrifying when he went purple in the face and the veins on his forehead stood out. All the same, it definitely was a ghost and this was the important thing. Although George was in human shape, Bertrand could see right through him and you couldn't do that with people, no matter how thin they were.

There was a smile on Bertrand's lips as he gently closed the door again, all thoughts of the flour forgotten. Now he had far more important things to think about.

* * *

After Mr Merryfellow had gone to bed, George was at a loose end. There was no Fenella to visit and none of the other things he normally did at night appealed to him. He did practise a few terrifying faces in front of the mirror but even George could see that they simply made him look ridiculous. Lying in the freezer wasn't any better. Although it was as cool and restful as ever, George wasn't really in the mood to rest.

Of course, George knew exactly what the trouble was. It was Bertrand. His arrival had upset George's routine. He hadn't been able to do a lot of the things he usually did with Mr Merryfellow.

Besides, George didn't like Bertrand as much as Mr Merryfellow seemed to and this wasn't simply because he was jealous. George had been watching Bertrand very carefully and he didn't think he was a nice little boy at all. He suspected that Bertrand was a rather nasty little boy who was simply pretending to be nice. Take the incident at Mrs Crumpet's tea shop, for example. Although George couldn't understand why anybody should be frightened of such a tiny animal, he was almost positive that Bertrand had let the mouse loose on purpose. And there was also the question of why Mr and Mrs Buckle had suddenly sent their son to stay with Matthew. It could be that Bertrand was such a nuisance, his parents had simply wanted to get rid of him for a little while.

George hadn't mentioned any of his doubts to

Mr Merryfellow. He knew how pleased Matthew was to have his nephew staying with him and George didn't want to spoil his friend's pleasure. He just hoped Bertrand wouldn't spoil it for him. George promised himself that he would continue to keep a very careful eye on Bertrand for the rest of his stay.

Now was as good a time as any to start. Bertrand should be asleep and this would give George a chance to have a good look through the things he had brought with him. There might be other surprises apart from Squeak. In any case, George had a selfish reason as well. He had wanted to try on Bertrand's school cap ever since he had first seen it.

No sooner had the thought entered George's head than he was floating up through the ceiling towards Bertrand's bedroom. As he had expected, the boy was fast asleep, eyes closed, his breathing deep and even. There was no danger of George being seen as long as he remained invisible.

Rather disappointingly, there was nothing in the suitcase apart from clothes. George wasn't to know that Mr and Mrs Buckle had been through it already and removed everything which shouldn't have been there. This was why the suitcase was only half full.

The pockets of Bertrand's jacket proved to be far more rewarding. For a start, there were several glass capsules filled with a yellowish liquid, each of them with the label STINK BOMB. George didn't have any idea what they were for but when he held one up to his nose, he discovered that it smelled rather like his mother when she was doing one of her really scary haunts. In another pocket there was a short forked stick with a piece of elastic attached to it, three conkers, several lengths of string, some marbles, a couple of pieces of well-chewed chewing-gum and a small box labelled ITCHING POWDER. George wondered whether to go and sprinkle some on Mr Merryfellow while he was asleep. His friend was always complaining of itchy skin and the powder might make him feel better. Bertrand had probably got the powder from the doctor for his own itchy skin.

Apart from a grubby handkerchief and Squeak, there was nothing else in the pockets. This meant that George could turn his attention to the cap. It was a truly splendid piece of headwear, green and gold with a large embossed badge. George had fallen in love with it immediately. He had been sure it would suit him far better than it did Bertrand and, to his delight, it fitted him perfectly when he tried it on.

'Ghost.'

For an instant George thought his ears must be playing tricks on him. Then Bertrand spoke again.

'Ghost, what are you doing with my cap?'

This time there could be no mistake and

George hastily snatched the cap from his head, dropping it on the floor. He even looked down to check that he was still invisible.

'You might as well answer me, George. I know you're there.'

But George didn't answer him. He was already floating from the room, travelling so fast that he didn't even pause to wonder how Bertrand knew his name. All he could think of was what Mr Merryfellow had told him about staying hidden from his nephew. George was certain that Matthew wouldn't be at all pleased when Bertrand told him what had happened.

Four

'Did you have a good night's sleep, Matthew?'

'Excellent, thank you, George.'

Mr Merryfellow cautiously tested the cup of tea which George had brought up to him in bed. Tea-making wasn't one of the things that ghosts did best. In fact, it wasn't at all unusual for George to forget to put in the tea-bag or to use water straight from the tap. On one never-to-be-forgotten morning, George had used salt instead of sugar and forgotten to switch on the gas when he had boiled the kettle. It had been rather like drinking brown seawater and the taste stayed in Mr Merryfellow's mouth all day.

This time, however, George had remembered to do everything properly and Mr Merryfellow sipped the tea gratefully.

'You weren't disturbed at all during the night, were you?' George asked.

'Why? Should I have been?'

For some reason George was all of a dither and Mr Merryfellow wondered why.

'I just thought Bertrand might have been in to see you.'

'As far as I know he's still fast asleep. I haven't seen hide nor hair of him since he went to bed last night.'

George heaved a sigh of relief but he knew there was still plenty of time for Bertrand to say something before he left for school. Until he did, George stayed very close to him. He was hovering invisibly beside Bertrand when he climbed out of bed and went into the bathroom to wash and do his hair. He was still with him thirty seconds later when Bertrand came out again. Washing had consisted of wiping a damp flannel across his face and using the same flannel to rub his teeth. He had combed his hair with his fingers.

Breakfast was the worst time, when Bertrand was sitting at the table with Mr Merryfellow, but George needn't have worried. Bertrand never talked while he was eating. Making mischief used up a lot of energy and Bertrand was a hearty eater. He was also very fast, using both his fork and knife to shovel food into his mouth. If he had tried to speak, he would have showered the entire room with a mixture of half-chewed sausage, egg and baked beans.

Half an hour after breakfast, Mr Merryfellow had left Bertrand at the school gates and there had still been no mention of ghosts trying on caps during the night. This made George feel a lot happier. Perhaps he wouldn't have to explain to Mr Merryfellow after all.

By the time Bertrand went to bed that night, George was almost back to his normal, cheerful self. It seemed that Bertrand had forgotten all about the incident of the previous night. Either that, or he must think it had been a dream. All the same, being caught by Bertrand still troubled George's conscience.

'Matthew,' he said suddenly. 'Why didn't you want Bertrand to know about me?'

'It's like I told you, George. He wouldn't understand.'

To tell the truth, there were occasions when Mr Merryfellow wasn't sure he understood himself.

'Couldn't you explain to him, though? Tell him how I came here and how we became friends.'

'I suppose I could.' Mr Merryfellow sounded dubious. 'It isn't really Bertrand that's the trouble, though. Boys his age are adaptable. They're quite used to grown-ups behaving strangely. The problems would come when he told other people about us.'

'Couldn't you say it was a secret? Make him promise not to tell.'

'That would be like telling him to lie and I couldn't do that.' Mr Merryfellow was as honest as the day was long. 'I'd much rather carry on the way we are.'

Normally George would have let the matter rest

but his conscience was troubling him even more after what Mr Merryfellow had said about lying.

'What problems would there be if other people knew about us?' he asked. 'I mean, I can understand people thinking it was strange. Lots of ghosts think the same about me when they hear we're friends instead of me haunting you. None of them causes me any problems, though.'

Mr Merryfellow laughed. 'Ghosts are different from human beings,' he explained. 'All ghosts know that there are human beings but not all human beings believe in ghosts. In fact, a lot of them still wouldn't believe in ghosts if one jumped up and bit them. If that kind of person learned that I'd said I was living with a ghost, they'd think I'd gone soft in the head. They might even have me locked up in the booby hatch.'

'What's the booby hatch?'

Now George was really concerned. He didn't realize that his friend wasn't being entirely serious.

'It's the place where they put people who are sick in the head,' Mr Merryfellow explained. 'That's the very last place I want to end up.'

'But Bertrand would be able to say that there really was a ghost.'

'People would think he was lying. Grown-ups hardly ever believe children unless they say what grown-ups want to hear.'

The conversation had done nothing at all to ease George's conscience. If anything, he felt worse than he had before. He hadn't really understood about the booby hatch but it sounded like a terrifying place and George wouldn't like to be responsible for his friend ending up there. It was just as well for George's peace of mind that he didn't know Bertrand had sneaked downstairs again and overheard the entire conversation.

How do you catch a ghost? This was the question which had been bothering Bertrand ever since he had learned about George. If it had been a mouse, say, it would have been easy. Even if there had been a tiger in the house, Bertrand would have known what to do. He could tie Uncle Matthew to his bed and put superglue on the floor so that when the tiger came to eat him up it would be stuck.

Ghosts were trickier, though. George obviously didn't want to talk to Bertrand, otherwise he would have answered when he was spoken to. Bertrand realized he had to do something more but he wasn't sure what. How could you catch something which was invisible and could drift through walls?

His first day at Gigglesworth School was also the first time Bertrand had ever been into a library without somebody forcing him to go. He spent almost the entire lunch hour in the school library but he couldn't find anything to help solve his problems. Although there were books on volcanoes and farming and spiders, there was nothing at all on how to catch a ghost. He obviously wasn't going to get any help from books.

For a while, Bertrand toyed with the idea of simply walking into the living room one night when his uncle was talking to George. This would be easy enough to do but unfortunately it didn't really suit Bertrand's plans. The last thing he wanted was for Uncle Matthew to know that Bertrand had discovered his secret. Bertrand didn't want to share George with anyone. He wanted to have a ghost of his very own. Bertrand had already decided that when he went back to London at the end of the holiday, he would be taking George with him.

After a second night with his ear pressed to the living-room door, Bertrand thought he knew how to make George do as he wanted. First, though, he still had to catch his ghost. Somehow or other he had to make George come when he called and, for the moment, there didn't seem to be any answer to the problem.

It was something which Bertrand thought about all week long and it affected him at school. By Friday, all the staff at Gigglesworth School had agreed that Bertrand Buckle was the naughtiest, worst-behaved child they had ever had the misfortune to teach. The mere mention of his name made them pale and nervous and several of them had already developed twitches. However, if Mr Whackem had been there, he would have been amazed at how well Bertrand was behaving. For, although he did manage to land himself in plenty of trouble, it was as much carelessness as anything.

On Tuesday, for example, Bertrand's class did science. They were learning about soil and the teacher asked the children to make up some experiments of their own. Although Toby Tattle had to have two days off and his mother came into school to complain to the headmaster, Bertrand honestly couldn't understand what all the fuss was about. In fact, he was very angry with Toby for getting him into so much trouble. The thing was, when Bertrand did an experiment, he liked to do it properly. All the other kids did really soppy experiments, like how much a bucket of soil weighed and how many worms they could find. As he told old Beaky, how was he supposed to discover how much soil you needed to bury somebody unless you actually tried it?

'But dear Toby nearly choked,' Mr Beak said sternly. 'You filled his mouth with earth.'

'That was his fault, sir.'

'What do you mean it was his fault? You put a spadeful of soil into his mouth.'

'If he hadn't been screaming so much, his silly

mouth wouldn't have been open. Then the earth couldn't have gone in.'

Mr Beak groaned. Like most grown-ups, he found talking to Bertrand similar to banging his head hard against a brick wall. It gave him a bad headache.

'What about his clothes then?' Mr Beak demanded. 'They were completely ruined.'

'That was Toby Tattle's fault too, sir.'

'How could it be his fault?' Mr Beak's voice had risen to a shriek. 'You buried the poor child.'

'I told him to take off his clothes, sir, but he didn't want to help with my experiment so I had to tie him up. When I tried to take his clothes off myself, the knots were in the way.'

After this, Mr Beak didn't waste any more time talking. Instead, he got straight down to business with his cane. As Bertrand had suspected, Mr Beak used the cane very effectively and Bertrand's bottom was still a bit sore when he was caned again on Thursday. Although he didn't say so, Bertrand thought this was a bit unfair. He had only been trying to make the fire drill a bit more realistic when he had set fire to the wastepaper basket. He hadn't known the curtains would catch light as well and that the Fire Brigade would have to be called.

Despite these misadventures, it was while Bertrand was at school that the solution to his problems came to him. In fact, it happened on

41

Friday afternoon during the art lesson. The class were all making signs and notices and Bertrand was quite proud of his: written in large, blood-red letters, it said DANJUR. SHARCS IN THE SWIMING PULE. Bertrand thought this was quite effective and he was busy with a picture at the top, showing a little girl being bitten in half by a shark, when the idea came to him. It was a marvellous, wonderful idea, one of the best Bertrand had ever had and he just knew it would work.

'That ghost will have to talk to me then,' he said to himself as he coloured the water around the little girl red. 'He won't dare not to.'

For once in his life Bertrand could hardly wait to go to bed.

Ever since he had been caught with the cap, George had steered well clear of Bertrand's room at night. Although Mr Merryfellow's nephew seemed to have completely forgotten the incident, George didn't want to risk any more accidents.

Although George missed Fenella's company, he seldom had any difficulty filling in the night-time hours. He simply did the things most ghosts did when they weren't haunting. For a start, the *Ghost Gazette* was delivered every night and George always enjoyed reading it. 'Hints for Haunts' was his favourite section but he also enjoyed doing the 'Spot the Head' competition. As a youngster, George had had a lot of practice finding his

father's head for him so he was quite good at
it.

Once the newspaper was finished, George often
drifted down into the village to have a look
around. Like most ghosts, he was fascinated by
the strange things human beings did. Take
Anthea Armpit, for example. George wasn't quite
sure but he thought she was practising to be a
ghost while she was still alive. Every night before
going bed, she twisted her hair into tight little
spikes, which stuck up from her head, and
smeared mud on her face to make a hideous
mask. George thought she looked quite frightening and he was especially impressed with the
way she took her teeth out, putting them in a glass
beside the bed. This might not be as effective as
carrying your head under your arm but it wasn't
at all bad for a human. It certainly made Mr
Armpit shudder when he looked at her.

Then there was poor Mr Pate who was going
bald. Every night he carefully spread hair restorer
on the bald patches and every night, when he was
asleep, his cat, Tiddles, came in and licked it off
again. Mr Pate kept getting balder and balder but
Tiddles was the hairiest cat in Gigglesworth.

George had intended to go down into the
village on Friday night. Mr Merryfellow was safely
in bed and George was about to leave when he
heard the sound of a door opening and closing
upstairs.

'It's Bertrand,' George thought to himself. 'I wonder what mischief he's up to at this time of night.'

Silently and invisibly, George floated upstairs. Although it was nearly midnight, light from Bertrand's bedroom was spilling out under the crack at the bottom of the door, illuminating a small patch of carpet on the landing outside.

'He should be asleep.' George was still talking to himself. 'Perhaps he's ill.'

George was just wondering whether he ought to tell Mr Merryfellow when he noticed a piece of white paper stuck to the outside of the bedroom door. He was certain that it hadn't been there when he had gone past a few minutes earlier. Drifting closer, George could see that it was a notice. 'GOST' it said, in the same blood-red letters which Bertrand had used at school, 'CUM AND SPEKE TO ME OR IT WIL BE WURS FOR UNKLE MATHUW. REEMEMBUR THE BUBY HATCH. BERTRAND.'

It took George a moment or two to work out what the message said. Once he had, he realized that Bertrand hadn't forgotten about him after all.

'I ought to tell Matthew. That's the best thing to do.'

George was in the freezer. This was the place he always went to when he was upset.

'But if I wake Matthew up, he'll be angry. He's always grumpy when he's disturbed during the night. Besides, he told me to stay hidden from Bertrand.'

The trouble was, there didn't seem to be many alternatives. George moved a packet of fish fingers to make himself more comfortable while he gave the matter some thought.

'The notice said it would be the worse for Matthew if I didn't do what Bertrand wanted.' Like most ghosts, George was used to talking to himself. It came from spending so much time on his own. 'It said something about the booby hatch but I don't think Bertrand would do anything nasty to his own uncle.'

George paused for a moment.

'Yes, I do,' he decided. 'Bertrand is a nasty, little boy. He enjoys doing nasty things.'

Mr Merryfellow had received a letter from Mr Beak complaining about Bertrand's behaviour at school. Mr Merryfellow might have made excuses for his nephew but George hadn't. Although he couldn't understand why anybody should be upset about being buried, Mr Beak's report had only served to confirm George's poor opinion of Bertrand. He didn't trust Bertrand at all.

'I mustn't let him do anything to hurt Matthew.' This was the most important thing as far as George was concerned. 'If Bertrand already knows I'm in the house, it can't do any harm to speak to him. I might be able to talk some sense into him.'

Although George wasn't too sure about the talking sense part, going to see Bertrand did seem to be the only answer. At the very least, George could find out what he wanted.

Reluctantly, George left the freezer and floated upstairs. The notice was still on Bertrand's door and for a moment the little ghost hesitated. It might be the sensible thing to do but George didn't want to talk to Bertrand. Mr Merryfellow was the only human George had ever spoken to and he was very different from his nephew. George was certain that Bertrand had something unpleasant in store for him.

'Come on, George,' he said, trying to buck himself up. 'Bertrand can't eat you.'

He floated through the door and into the bedroom. The light was still on and Bertrand was wide awake. He was laying on his back, hands clasped behind his head while he stared up at the ceiling. He looked as though he was prepared to wait all night and the little smile on his lips only increased George's uneasiness. Not for the first time, George wished he was a proper haunting ghost. Then Bertrand would have been too scared of him to attempt anything unpleasant.

'I'm here,' George said in a small voice.

'It's about time.'

Bertrand removed his hands from behind his

head and looked around the bedroom. As George was invisible, he couldn't see him.

'Where are you?' he asked.

'Over here by the wardrobe.'

'Let's have a look at you then.'

By now, George was convinced that he had made a bad mistake but it was far too late to back out. Nervously, he did as Bertrand had instructed and made himself visible. Although he had seen George before, Bertrand was still disappointed. He had hoped that George would be a bit more terrifying close to.

'You're not much, are you?' Bertrand said. 'I thought ghosts were supposed to be frightening.'

'Most of us are.'

'So what went wrong with you?'

George shifted uncomfortably and didn't answer. Bertrand had hit on a sensitive point.

'I suppose you'll have to do. Your name is George, isn't it?'

'That's right.'

'Well, George, you and I are going to come to an agreement.'

Bertrand was thoroughly enjoying himself. Things were working out just as he had planned.

'What sort of an agreement?'

'It will work like this. I shan't tell anybody about Uncle Matthew living with a ghost and you'll do everything I say.'

Although Bertrand wasn't very good at reading and writing and things like that, in some ways he was quite clever.

'What sort of things will I have to do?'

'Everything I say.'

'I won't do anything bad like stealing or hurting anybody.'

'That's all right. I'll just want you to help me with a few jokes.'

That was all to begin with anyway. Getting his own back on Toby Tattle and Mr Beak would just be the start. Bertrand would mention the part about going back with him to London later.

'What kind of jokes will they be?'

'That's for me to decide.'

George nodded his head. 'Can I go now?'

His mind was already made up. George would go and stay in Fenella's crypt until Bertrand had left for home. He could explain to Mr Merryfellow afterwards. Unfortunately, it was as though Bertrand could read his mind.

'It won't do any good you hiding or going away,' he said. 'I'll still tell people about Uncle Matthew and he'll be sent straight to the booby hatch. If anybody asks him, he'll have to tell the truth. You know he never tells lies.'

'Oh.'

'Besides, you're going to make me a promise, ghost. Say this after me. I promise to do everything Bertrand tells me.'

48

'I promise to do everything Bertrand tells me.'

George's voice was so small that Bertrand could hardly hear it.

'And not to tell anybody Bertrand is making me do it.'

Once again, George repeated the words.

'There's no need to look so miserable, ghost,' Bertrand told him. 'We're going to have lots of fun together. You can clear off now but I expect you back first thing in the morning for your instructions.'

George agreed and then drifted from the room, feeling more miserable then ever. Bertrand, however, was absolutely delighted. He still had a big smile on his face when he fell asleep.

Five

'I have to do some shopping this morning, Bertrand. Do you want to come with me?'

Breakfast was over and Mr Merryfellow was trying to get the day sorted out.

'No thank you, Uncle.'

'I suppose it wouldn't be very exciting for a lad your age. What plans have you made?'

'I thought I'd go down to the river.'

'That's a good idea. It's very popular with the local boys in the summer. No doubt you've arranged to meet up with some of your new chums from school.'

'I might bump into one or two of them.'

It was easier for Bertrand to say this than to admit that he didn't have any chums. This wasn't simply because he was new to Gigglesworth. He just wasn't the sort of boy who made many friends. Even when somebody did like Bertrand, it wasn't long before a grown-up interfered. Bertrand wasn't the kind of boy any parent

50

wanted their child to have as a friend. All the same, he had been telling the truth when he said that he hoped to meet some of the boys from school. Today was the day Bertrand intended to have his revenge on Toby Tattle. He had overheard Toby arranging to meet two of his friends at the river.

'How about you, George?' Mr Merryfellow asked after Bertrand had left the room. 'Are you coming with me?'

'I don't think so.'

Although Bertrand was no longer there, George remained invisible. He didn't want his friend to see how embarrassed he was.

'Oh.' Mr Merryfellow was disappointed. He enjoyed his Saturday morning excursions with George. 'What are you doing then.'

'I thought I'd keep an eye on Bertrand for you. Make sure he doesn't get into any more trouble.'

'What a good idea. You really are a thoughtful little fellow, George.'

Mr Merryfellow felt quite proud of George. Fancy giving up his trip to the shops so he could look after Bertrand! He wasn't to know that George hadn't any choice in the matter. Bertrand had said he wanted George to go with him and that meant George had to go whether he wanted to or not.

* * *

Bertrand was enjoying himself, although the cows in the fields behind Mr Merryfellow's house weren't nearly so happy. All they wanted to do was eat grass and chew the cud like they normally did. They certainly didn't want to be chased around the field by somebody pretending to be a cowboy, especially when it was so close to milking time.

At first, Bertrand hadn't been too successful rounding them up because there were too many cows for him to handle on his own. As soon as he had one cow where he wanted it, two others would wander off to another part of the meadow. However, it was much better once he made George help him. Cows didn't like ghosts at all. George hovered invisibly to one side of the herd, shouting at any cows which tried to break away, while Bertrand moved them in the direction he wanted. It wasn't very long before he had them all neatly penned in one corner of the field.

Once he had them there, Bertrand wasn't sure what to do next. In all the films he had seen, the cowboys branded the cattle after the round-up but Bertrand didn't have a fire and he didn't have anything to brand with. The pencil he had in his pocket wasn't any good. Although it wrote on paper, it didn't even make a mark on a cow's skin. He was just wondering whether his penknife would be any better when they were inter-rupted.

'Oy.'

The loud, indignant voice belonged to a burly, red-faced man. He was standing on the far side of the field and waving a large stick in Bertrand's direction.

'Who's that?' Bertrand asked.

'It's Farmer Giles,' George told him. 'He doesn't sound very pleased to me.'

This didn't surprise Bertrand – hardly any grown-ups sounded pleased when they were talking to him. All the same, he couldn't understand why the farmer was so upset. Nobody ever shouted at the cowboys on television when they rounded up the cattle. There were times when Bertrand found other human beings almost as hard to understand as George did.

'Oy.' Farmer Giles had started to run across the field and he sounded angrier than ever. 'What do you think you're doing with my cows, you young hooligan?'

There were certain things which Bertrand did understand very well indeed. One of them was that when a grown-up sounded as angry as Farmer Giles and was waving a stick, the sensible thing to do was head in the opposite direction as fast as possible.

'Come on,' he said to George. 'Let's get out of here.'

Bertrand didn't stop running before he had put another field between himself and the irate farmer. Only then, when he was safely hidden behind a hedge, did he turn to see what was happening behind him. Farmer Giles had long since given up the chase and, to Bertrand's amazement, he was doing exactly what Bertrand himself had been doing, herding the cattle together.

'Selfish old fool,' Bertrand muttered angrily. 'He wanted to do the round-up himself.'

'He does it every day at this time,' George explained. 'He takes the cows to be milked.'

'What do you mean?'

Bertrand was a city boy, ignorant of the ways of the country. As he never ever listened to his teachers, he was ignorant about almost everything else as well.

'He takes the cows into a shed and gets the milk out of them.'

'Don't be so silly, ghost. Milk comes out of bottles.'

'It comes out of cows first before it goes into bottles. There are some bits hanging underneath the cows. You pull them and the milk comes squirting out.'

Farmer Giles was the old-fashioned type who didn't believe in machines. All his cows were still milked by hand.

'Get along with you,' Bertrand sneered. 'You're pulling my leg.'

'I haven't touched your leg.'

Bertrand laughed.

'I meant that you're fibbing to me.'

'No I'm not. Ghosts never lie. If you don't believe me, you can ask your uncle.'

This time Bertrand didn't argue. Now George had mentioned it, he seemed to remember somebody at school saying something about cows and milk. Besides, Bertrand had stood up and could see into the next field.

'How did you say the milk comes out?' he asked. 'You just pull at the bits underneath and the milk squirts out?'

'That's right.'

'Don't the cows mind?'

'They seem to enjoy it.'

'Well, we'll soon see if you're right,' Bertrand said, starting to push his way through the hedge. 'I'm going to milk this cow here before that farmer remembers he's left it behind.'

When George floated up to look over the hedge, he could see that there was a cow on its own in the next field. At least, it looked very much like a cow but there was something different about it.

'Bertrand,' he said nervously. 'I'm not sure that's the right kind of cow.'

'What do you mean, ghost?' Bertrand stopped halfway through the hedge. 'It's got horns on top of its head, hasn't it? It can't be a horse or dog.'

'It looks different to me. Besides, there's a ring in its nose.'

'Perhaps it's going to a fancy dress party. Come on. Otherwise we'll be late getting to the river.'

Bertrand impatiently pushed his way through the hedge and started across the field towards the cow with the ring in its nose. George floated reluctantly after him. He still couldn't work out exactly what was wrong with this particular cow but he just knew there was something.

Basil was Farmer Giles's prize bull. For a bull he was exceptionally placid and good tempered, a lazy animal who far preferred eating grass to getting angry. This was why he didn't pay too much attention when he saw Bertrand come into the field. The boy wasn't doing anything to annoy Basil so Basil was prepared to leave him alone. Even when Bertrand came right up to him, the bull continued to munch grass.

'Right,' Bertrand said, rubbing his hands together. 'What part do I pull to get the milk out?'

'It's called the others,' George told him.

He had heard Farmer Giles use the word while he was at work in his milking shed. At least, it was the word George thought he had heard him use.

'And these others are underneath the cow?'

'They should be.'

Bertrand walked all round the bull, searching for something which looked as though it might have milk inside. Basil was keeping one watchful eye on him as he did so. The boy was beginning to irritate him a little. All this attention was disturbing his morning feed.

'There's nothing that looks like others to me,' Bertrand announced after he had walked round the bull twice.

'I can't see them either,' George admitted. 'Like I said before, I think it's the wrong kind of cow.'

This was something Bertrand thought about for a moment or two. Although George knew more about cows than he did, Bertrand wasn't the type of boy who gave up easily.

'If it's a different kind of cow,' he said, half speaking to himself, 'there must be a different way of getting the milk out.'

He began walking around the bull once more, stopping every now and again to prod at parts which particularly interested him. The one part of Basil that Bertrand didn't examine was his eyes which was a shame. If he had, Bertrand would have noticed that they were taking on a reddish tinge. Basil was beginning to remember that he was a bull and that bulls were big, fierce animals who didn't let themselves be poked and prodded by little boys. He had actually stopped feeding which was always a danger sign.

'I've got it,' Bertrand said, smiling happily. 'This must be a pump-action cow. You have to pump the milk out. That's probably why it's kept on its own. Pump-action cows in one field, ordinary cows in another.'

'What do you pump?'

George wasn't sure that Bertrand had the right answer.

'Its tail, silly. You pump the tail up and down and the milk comes squirting out underneath. You watch.'

Bertrand walked behind Basil, grabbed hold of his tail and began pumping it up and down vigorously. For an instant, Basil couldn't believe what was happening to him. He was so outraged that he couldn't move.

'Is any milk coming out?' Bertrand asked.

'Not yet.'

'Perhaps you have to pull the tail, not pump it.'

Taking hold of the bull's tail with both hands, Bertrand tugged as hard as he could and this was the final straw as far as Basil was concerned. With an ear-shattering bellow, he pulled himself free and swung round to face his tormentor. Farmer Giles wouldn't have recognized him any more. His eyes were blood-red with rage, steam was being puffed from his nostrils and he was pawing at the ground with one front hoof.

'Ghost,' Bertrand said, his voice trembling. 'I don't think this cow likes being milked.'

Then Bertrand was running for his life with

Basil in hot pursuit. Luckily for Bertrand, he had an advantage. He was used to running away from people who were angry with him and he was very good at it. Basil, on the other hand, hadn't broken out of a walk for years. Angry as he was and hard as he tried, there was nothing he could do to stop the boy getting further and further ahead of him.

Poor Bertrand had no idea that he was winning the race because he didn't dare waste time by looking back over his shoulder. He could hear the angry snorts and the heavy footsteps and they sounded as though they were just behind him. All Bertrand wanted to do was reach the hedge and be safe from the maddened beast which was chasing him. When he arrived at the hedge, he didn't even bother to look for a gap. He simply dived into it and started wriggling, ignoring the prickles and branches that scratched him.

For a moment, it looked as though Bertrand was going to make it because he was almost as good at wriggling as he was at running. His head was safely through the hedge, and his shoulders, but then the belt of his trousers snagged on a branch. No matter how much Bertrand twisted and turned, he couldn't free himself, which meant his lower half was still on the wrong side of the hedge.

Until he saw that Bertrand was stuck, Basil had given up the chase. He had almost slowed to a walk before he realized what had happened. The top part of the horrid little boy might have disappeared but his bottom was still framed invitingly by the hedge. Taking his time now, Basil walked up to the hedge to investigate. He was still very angry indeed and the bottom really did look most inviting. Basil lowered his head and prodded it experimentally with one horn. There was a lovely squishing sensation as it dug in.

'Ow,' Bertrand yelled. 'Do something to help me, ghost.'

George wasn't sure exactly what he could do. He knew he wasn't nearly strong enough to pull Bertrand free from the hedge. While he hesitated, Basil tested out the other horn. The squishy sensation was even more pleasant than it had been the first time.

'OOOWWW!' If he had been able to, Bertrand would have liked to clap both hands to his injured bottom. 'That cow is turning my posterior into a pin-cushion.'

Nice as it had been, Basil didn't consider this to be punishment enough. He was too close to the wriggling boy to use his horns properly. It would be much, much better if he had a run-up. Then he would really teach the little monster what happened to nasty boys who pulled his tail. Why, he could knock him halfway to the moon. Happily, the bull moved back from the hedge. He hadn't had this much fun for years.

It was fortunate for Bertrand that George realized what was about to happen. However much he disliked Bertrand, he couldn't simply float by and allow him to be hurt. Mr Merryfellow would never forgive him.

'Try and undo your belt,' George called out to Bertrand, already moving after Basil. 'I'll keep the cow away from you.'

By now Basil had reached a suitable place to begin his run-up and was taking careful aim.

'When I've finished with that little beast,' he thought to himself, 'he won't be able to sit down for a year.'

Basil was just about to begin his charge when, to his amazement, he felt another sharp tug on his tail. Swinging round, he could hardly believe that there was a second tail-tugger in his field. Basil was so enraged he hardly noticed that there was something strange about this one, that he was so shadowy it was possible to see right through him.

'Come on, you silly old cow,' George taunted him. 'Let's see what you can do with me.'

There was no need for a second invitation. With a bellow of rage which could be heard for miles around, Basil lowered his head and charged at George. He was halfway across the field before he realized that somehow or other he had missed. It was almost as though he had run straight through the second boy. With a snort of rage, Basil turned to see where he was.

'I'm over here,' George called out. 'Surely you can do better than that.'

By now, Basil had forgotten all about the boy stuck in the hedge. It was George he was after and the ghost was now floating in front of the large oak tree in the middle of the field, waving cheerfully at Basil. The bull was determined not to miss again. This time he kept his eye on George all the way when he charged, ready to change direction if his tormentor tried to get out of his way. But George didn't. He simply stayed where he was, still smiling cheerfully.

'I'll show him,' Basil thought. 'I'll teach him to mess around with me.'

Unfortunately, nobody had told poor Basil about ghosts. It wasn't until he hit the oak tree with such force that acorns came showering down on his head that he realized his mistake. By then it was too late. When Basil tried to see where George had gone to, he couldn't move his head. Both his horns were firmly embedded in the tree trunk.

'Never mind,' George said from beside Basil, after he had checked the bull was all right. 'You'll soon set yourself free.'

By this time Bertrand was safely on the far side of the hedge. Apart from the odd twig sticking out of his hair and a couple of rips in his trousers, he was none the worse for his adventure.

'Thanks, ghost,' he said when George joined him. 'You did a good job.'

'I didn't do it for you,' George told him. 'I did it for your uncle.'

Now he had had a chance to think about it, George would have quite liked to see Basil punish Bertrand a little.

'Do you know something, ghost.' Bertrand hadn't really been listening to George. He was too busy peering over the hedge. 'I could have another go at milking that cow while it's stuck.'

'I wouldn't if I were you.'

As if to prove George's point, there was the sound of cracking wood as Basil pulled one of his horns free. It wouldn't be long before the other one was free as well.

'Maybe you're right. Come on, ghost. Let's go down to the river.'

Bertrand set off at a run. He was no coward but a cow which was angry enough to attack a tree might not be put off by a mere hedge.

Six

It was a warm morning and running away from Farmer Giles and the cow had made Bertrand hot and sticky. The cool, clear water of the river seemed very tempting to him. Toby Tattle and his two friends certainly looked as though they were enjoying themselves, leaping around and splashing in the pool. Bertrand stood back among the trees while he watched them, feeling rather jealous. He had never played in a river in his life. Nor had he ever been anywhere you didn't have to wear a swimming costume.

'Are they swimming?'

The question made Bertrand jump. He wasn't used to George yet. It still startled him when a voice spoke out of thin air.

'No, not really,' he answered. 'They're just fooling around.'

'But they're in the water.'

'Swimming is when you move along in the water without touching the bottom.'

'Oh.' George thought he understood now. 'Can you swim?'

'Sort of.'

What Bertrand did best was sink. He had only been allowed to go to one swimming lesson at school. After he had experimented to see how long Samantha Squat could breathe under water, Bertrand had been stopped from going any more. Mr Whackem said Bertrand had been trying to drown her and he hadn't listened when Bertrand had tried to explain that he would have let go of Samantha's head as soon as the bubbles stopped coming out of her mouth. It just wasn't fair. Teachers were always telling children to try to find things out for themselves but when he did try, Bertrand usually ended up in trouble.

'Are you going swimming today?' George asked.

'I don't know.'

Although Bertrand had come to the river intending mischief, he wasn't so sure now. Toby and his friends really did appear to be having fun. A rope was hung in the branches of a tree beside the river. The boys would swing themselves out before allowing themselves to drop into the water below with a great splash.

'If I ask them nicely,' Bertrand thought, 'perhaps they might let me play too.'

At first the boys in the river didn't see Bertrand when he walked down to the riverbank opposite to where the rope was hanging. Toby Tattle was busy climbing into the tree and his two friends were watching him.

'Toby,' Bertrand called out. 'Toby Tattle.'

Three heads swung in Bertrand's direction. None of the faces looked pleased to see him.

'What do you want, Buckle?'

Toby's voice didn't sound friendly either. If he had been on his own, he would have been a bit frightened of Bertrand. With two of his friends to back him up, he felt quite brave.

'I'm sorry about what happened at school,' Bertrand said. 'It won't happen again. Can I come and play with you?'

'You must be joking. My mum says I'm not to have anything to do with you. Besides, I don't want to play with you. It's not safe. You'd probably drown one of us.'

'Please.'

'Not likely.'

As he spoke, Toby pushed himself out of the tree, holding firmly on to the rope. He pushed much harder than usual and, as he swung through the air, he came out with a Tarzan yell. For a moment Bertrand thought he was going to come right across the river but at the height of the swing, Toby let go of the rope, landing just in front of Bertrand. It was the biggest splash of the morning and nearly all the water went over Bertrand, drenching him from head to toe. The three boys in the river were all laughing and they joined together in splashing more water over Bertrand as he retreated from the bank. George was laughing too but as he was invisible, Bertrand didn't know.

'Rotten lot,' Bertrand muttered. 'Try to be nice and that's what happens. I'll show them.'

'Show them what?' George asked.

They were hidden from the river by trees now and Bertrand stopped to grin at where George's voice had come from.

'I'm going to show them what my ghost can do,' he said. 'That should teach them.'

Then he started to explain.

It was Toby Tattle's turn on the rope again and this was what George had been waiting for. When Toby reached the take-off branch and pulled the rope towards him, George was floating level with him. As the boy jumped from the branch and swung out towards the river, George seized hold of the rope with both ghostly hands and stopped it from swinging. Instead of sailing out over the water, Toby found himself suspended in mid-air, midway between the tree and the river. Neither Toby nor the boys below could understand what had happened.

'Stop hanging around up there,' Walter Winge shouted. 'What do you think you're doing?'

'I'm stuck. The rope just stopped swinging.'

'You didn't push off hard enough,' Percy Pratt suggested. 'Try swinging your legs.'

Toby swung his legs as hard as he could but the rope hardly moved. He was no nearer the tree or the river.

'I really am stuck.'

Now Toby was beginning to be a little bit frightened.

'Just let yourself drop. It's not far to the ground.'

It wasn't but when he looked, Toby could see there was a large patch of stinging nettles directly beneath him. They didn't look at all inviting.

'I'll be stung to death.'

'OK.' Walter was the practical one. 'If you just hang on, I'll climb up the tree and hook the rope back.'

'Hurry up, will you. My arms are beginning to stretch.'

'That's all right. You'll be able to scratch your ankles without bending down.'

Although Percy thought what he had said was quite amusing, he couldn't understand why Toby was laughing so much. Percy wasn't to know that George had let go of the rope and had started to tickle Toby's armpits.

'Ha, ha, ha,' Toby chortled. 'Ho, ho, ho. He, he, he.'

Having ghostly fingers tickle under your arms was far, far worse than being tickled on the soles of

69

the feet with a feather. Despite the nettles below him, Toby was laughing so much that it was impossible to keep hold of the rope.

'Ha, ha, ha, I'm slipping,' he chortled.

'Ho, ho, ho, I'm falling,' he spluttered.

'He, he, he, HELP,' he screeched.

To his watching friends, it was as though Toby had been transformed into a great, pink ball. Still standing in the water, they watched open-mouthed as he dropped from the rope, disappearing into the nettles before he leapt back high in the air, both hands clutched to his bottom.

'OOOWWW,' he yelled. 'I'm stung all over. OOOOOWWWWW.'

He landed clear of the nettles and started dancing around on the bank, moaning loudly. He really did look very funny, prancing around without any clothes on, and both Walter and Percy had to hide their smiles behind their hands. Over on the far bank, hidden among the trees, Bertrand was laughing so much he had fallen over.

It wasn't until Percy found some dock leaves for him that Toby began to feel better and even then he wasn't very happy. When his friends suggested going back into the river, he shook his head vigorously.

'The water will make my stings hurt again,' he said. 'I'm getting dressed and then I'm going home.'

70

He turned away and started towards where he had left his clothes. Then he stopped. His clothes were no longer there. For a moment he thought he must have been in the wrong place but when he looked around, they were nowhere in sight.

'Where are my clothes?' he demanded.

'And ours,' Walter and Percy said together.

All three piles of clothing had completely disappeared from the river bank.

George wasn't at all happy. Haunting human beings was one thing. That was only natural for a ghost but what Bertrand was making him do was very different. It was nasty and mean whatever Bertrand said, and George had tried to point this out.

'It's only a joke,' Bertrand had replied. 'It's just a bit of fun.'

'A joke is only a joke when it makes people laugh.'

'Well, it's going to make me laugh a lot so that's all right.'

'Those boys down there won't think it's funny,' George had retorted. 'They'll be frightened.'

'What's wrong with that? You ghosts are supposed to frighten people.'

'Not out of doors we aren't and not in broad daylight.'

'Perhaps you'll start a new fashion, ghost. Just remember what I told you to do and don't miss anything out. If you don't do a good job, poor old Uncle Matthew is on his way to the booby hatch.'

Bertrand had sounded as though he had meant what he said and George was left with no choice. He knew he had to follow Bertrand's instructions to the letter. First of all, he had sneaked down invisibly and removed the boys' clothes from the river bank, hiding them in some nearby bushes. This hadn't been too bad because it was rather like the games of hide-and-seek he played with Mr Merryfellow. However, George couldn't make any excuses about what he had done to Toby Tattle on the rope. Although the rope was so close to the ground and George had been as careful as possible, the boy could easily have hurt himself.

Now George was about to do something which was even worse. No ghost ever haunted during the hours of daylight without a special licence. It was against the rules. Besides, George didn't really want to frighten anybody without a reason. Although he would have liked to be frightening like other ghosts, he didn't particularly want to terrify human beings any more. George simply thought it would be rather nice to be able to terrify them if he ever felt like it.

'If it wasn't for Matthew, I wouldn't do it,' George muttered to himself, tying the laces of Toby Tattle's shoes. He was already wearing the rest of his clothes. 'And I'd tell Bertrand so as well.'

Unfortunately, Mr Merryfellow had to be considered and George knew it was up to him to protect him from the booby hatch. This was why George was dressing himself in Toby Tattle's clothes. He only had one shoe to lace up and then he would be ready.

By now Toby and his two friends had started to search among the bushes lining the river bank. Exactly what had happened to their clothes was still a mystery to them but Toby had his own theory.

'It was that Buckle brat,' he said. 'It must have been.'

'I don't know,' Walter said. 'He was on the other side of the river when we saw him.'

'It's easy enough to get across.'

'We'd have seen him, though. Our clothes were right out in the open.'

'It was Buckle all right.' Toby had his mind made up. 'Next you'll be telling me that my clothes walked off on their own.'

At that moment Toby's clothes walked out of the bushes on their own. At least, as George was invisible, it looked as though the clothes were walking by themselves. The boys didn't notice at first so George coughed politely.

'Excuse me,' he said. 'Were you looking for me?'

The boys couldn't believe their eyes or their ears. Horror-struck, they watched as Toby's clothes strolled across the grass towards them. Everything would have been normal except that there was no head above the collar, no hands at the ends of the sleeves and no legs between the trousers and socks. To the boys it looked as though the clothes had taken on a life of their own.

'Well, say something to me,' the clothes said to them. 'Aren't you pleased to find me?'

The short answer was no, they weren't. All three boys would rather have stayed naked than be confronted by clothes which moved around by themselves and could speak.

'P-p-please,' Toby Tattle stuttered. 'T-t-tell me I'm dr-dr-dreaming.'

'You're dr-dr-dreaming,' the clothes told him.

'N-n-no I'm n-n-not, a-a-am I?'

Toby looked at his friends but neither of them could speak. Both of them were shivering from head to toe, knees knocking and teeth chattering.

'If you won't come over here to fetch me, Toby Tattle,' the clothes said, 'I'll have to come over to you. Otherwise you're likely to catch a chill. You're shivering already.'

When George started moving towards them again, it was more than the frightened boys could stand. Suddenly all three of them found their tongues again.

'Cripes,' said Walter.

'Golly gosh,' said Percy.

'Gordon Bennett,' said Toby.

'HHHEEELLLPPP,' all three shouted together.

Then they had all turned and started to run, not knowing where they were going and not really caring as long as it was a long way away from the terrible talking clothes. Across the river they splashed and up the far bank. George hesitated for a moment before he went after them.

'Hey,' he shouted. 'Wait for me.'

They didn't. The sound of his voice made them run even faster and George had to put on a spurt of speed to catch up with them, floating along between Walter and Percy and slightly behind Toby. The boys were concentrating so hard on their running that they didn't realize he was there at first.

'Faster,' Toby panted. 'We mustn't let those clothes catch up with us.'

'Are we getting away from them?'

'I think so.'

'There aren't any clothes behind us,' George told them, still keeping pace.

Once again, the sound of George's voice had a miraculous effect. The boys thought they had been running as fast as they possibly could. Now they discovered that they hadn't been.

'Gordon Bennett,' yelled Walter, glancing to his right.

'Cripes,' yelled Percy, glancing to his left.

'Golly gosh,' yelled Toby, looking back over his shoulder.

'HHHEEELLLPPP,' all three boys shouted together.

Then they were running even faster than before, moving so fast that their legs were only a blur. Through the woods they galloped, paying no attention to the small stones which dug into their feet or the branches which whipped at their bare bodies. Escape was the only thought they had in their minds and they didn't even pay much attention when Bertrand appeared beside the track ahead of them. He was laughing so much that he had tears running down his cheeks.

'Faster, you wallies,' he shouted out to them. 'The clothes are catching up.'

Although George stopped chasing them once he was level with Bertrand, the boys didn't know this. On through the trees they raced, up the hill and down into the next valley. They were so frightened that they had forgotten about not having any clothes on. This was a shame because it was in the next valley that the 3rd Gigglesworth Brownie Pack was having its weekend camp.

The girls were all busy preparing their lunch and it was Toby Tattle's sister, Tania, who spotted them first.

'Brown Owl,' she said. 'My brother's coming.'
'Oh yes, dear.'

Miss Bun was busy preparing stew and she didn't raise her head. Apart from being Brown Owl, she also taught at Gigglesworth School.

'He's got two friends with him, Brown Owl. They're running ever so fast.'

'Fancy that, dear.'

'They're not wearing any clothes, Brown Owl.'

'That's nice, dear.'

Miss Bun added a pinch of salt and took a spoonful of the stew to test it for flavour. It was only when it was in her mouth that she realized what Tania had said.

'WHAT DID YOU SAY?' she shrieked, spraying the Brownies nearest to her with stew. 'WITH-OUT ANY CLOTHES ON?'

As soon as Miss Bun raised her head, she could see that Tania was right. The three boys were halfway down the hill by now, still running at top speed, and they clearly didn't have a stitch of clothing on. Although all the girls were laughing, apart from the ones who had been sprayed with stew, Miss Bun wasn't at all amused.

'Into the tents, girls,' she instructed. 'I'll deal with this.'

She shooed the girls into their tents and picked up the largest wooden spoon she had. Holding it firmly in her hand, she planted herself in the middle of the track.

'Keep away from here, you little beasts,' she shouted.

The boys didn't take any notice. Now they were closer, Miss Bun could see the terrified expressions on their faces.

'They're mad,' she said to herself. 'Stark, raving mad. The sun must have affected them.'

Toby was in the lead when the boys reached the camp and Miss Bun gave him a good, hard whack with the wooden spoon. Unfortunately, this wasn't enough to stop him. Toby behaved as though the Brown Owl wasn't there, running straight into her and knocking her flat on her back into the large puddle behind her. Before she could drag herself up again, Walter had arrived and he used her as a bridge as he ran over her. The last of the three was Percy and although he was the slowest, he was also the heaviest. As he ran over her, Miss Bun could feel herself being pressed deeper into the mud at the bottom of the puddle, so deep that she couldn't pull herself free. She had to lie where she was and listen to the boys' footsteps receding into the distance.

When the girls emerged from their tents a minute or two later, they had to help pull Miss Bun to her feet. She came out of the mud with a loud, plopping sound which did nothing to improve her temper.

'You're all wet, Brown Owl,' Tania Tattle said helpfully.

'Yes, dear.'

'There's muddy footprints all up your clothes.'

'I know, dear.'

'You look ever so funny, Brown Owl.'

This was when Miss Bun hit Tania Tattle with the wooden spoon she still had in her hand. As she did so, she noticed that there was a fourth boy at the top of the hill. This one had all his clothes on but he was rolling around on the floor kicking his legs delightedly in the air. Despite the distance, the sound of his laughter clearly reached the irate Brown Owl. She immediately recognized who it was.

'I don't have any idea what's been happening here,' Miss Bun said to herself, 'but I do know who was responsible, Bertrand Buckle. Just you wait until I tell Mr Beak on Monday.'

Up on the hill, Bertrand hadn't realized that the Brown Owl was one of the teachers from school. Or that Miss Bun had recognized him. He was far too delighted with the success of his prank to be bothered with details like this. Watching the scene below, he had laughed so much that his tummy was hurting.

'Oh, dear,' he said at last, clutching his aching stomach. 'You did well, ghost. Very well indeed.'

The compliment did nothing to cheer George up. He was still feeling ashamed of himself.

'Will the clothes be all right where we left them?' he asked.

'They'll be found.' Bertrand wasn't a bit

bothered about the clothes. All he could think about was the great times he would be able to have with a tame ghost to do his bidding. 'One thing's for sure. That Toby Tattle won't be tattling about me any more. We really showed him, didn't we?'

'Yes, I suppose we did.'

George said this rather sadly but Bertrand didn't notice.

'This morning was only a start, ghost. On Monday we're really going to have some fun.'

'What's going to happen then?'

'You're coming to school with me, ghost. You'll enjoy that.'

Although George didn't say anything, he was sure that Bertrand was wrong. George didn't think he would enjoy himself at all.

Seven

To begin with, it was George who was wrong. He did enjoy himself because being at Gigglesworth School brought back happy memories of his own years at the Academy of Ghosts. Some things were very different, of course, like the subjects which were studied. Bertrand studied history, not haunting, and general studies instead of ghostly screams but there were other things which were very similar. The daily assembly, for example, was almost exactly the same except that at the Academy it was always held at midnight, not nine o'clock in the morning. Mr Beak was just as boring and long-winded as George's own head-master, Mr Wraith, had been. Even the teachers sitting behind him on the stage looked as though they were falling asleep.

Although George had to remain invisible, he amused himself by pretending to be one of the pupils, floating cross-legged at the end of the same line Bertrand was in. Standing on the stage at the front of the hall, Mr Beak went on and on and on. And on and on and on. The boy sitting next to George had started snoring quietly and George would have liked to imitate him. The boy might not snore as loudly as Mr Merryfellow did when he was asleep but he made a nice bubbling sound, which George would have liked to practise.

It wasn't until the very end of the assembly that Mr Beak suddenly attracted everybody's attention.

'There's one final thing,' the headmaster said. 'Bertrand Buckle is to report to my office immediately after assembly.'

All the children knew at once what was going to happen to Bertrand – Mr Beak's tone of voice didn't leave any room for doubt – so it was only George who didn't understand. The cane wasn't ever used at the Academy of Ghosts. As young ghosts never misbehaved, there wasn't any need for it. In any case, a cane wouldn't be very effective on a ghostly bottom. It would simply pass straight through.

The only reason Mr Wraith had ever summoned a young ghost to his office was to congratulate him on a particularly good piece of work. George could still remember how proud he had felt when he had been praised the first time he had managed to float through a brick wall without getting stuck. He assumed that Bertrand must feel the same. He noticed that Bertrand seemed rather pale but George thought this must be because he was so pleased.

After the final hymn, all the other children filed out to their classes, leaving Bertrand to walk slowly towards the office on his own. At least, nearly on his own because George was floating by his side. He wanted to know what Bertrand had done to make Mr Beak praise him.

'Congratulations,' George whispered in his ear.

'Are you trying to be funny, ghost?' Bertrand demanded fiercely.

'What do you mean?'

George was puzzled.

'I'm in trouble,' Bertrand told him. 'You'd better stay close. I'm going to need you.'

A group of children was coming towards them so George couldn't ask any more questions until they were safely past. In fact, it wasn't until they were standing outside the door of Mr Beak's office that Bertrand was able to explain.

'I think I'm going to be caned,' he said.

'You mean you're going to be planted in the garden?'

The only canes George knew about were the ones Mr Merryfellow used for his runner beans.

'No, you idiot. Old Beaky is going to use a cane to beat me.'

'Are your trousers dusty then?'

George had once seen Mr Merryfellow beating a carpet.

'Of course not, ghost. It's a punishment.'

'Oh.' George still didn't really understand. 'Does it hurt?'

'That's the whole idea. When old Beaky has finished with me I'll be lucky if I can sit down for the rest of the day.'

Although George didn't say so, this sounded just what Bertrand deserved.

'What do you want me to do?' he asked.

'I'd have thought that was obvious. You've got to stop Beaky caning me.'

'How?'

There was no chance for Bertrand to answer because at that moment Mr Beak opened his office door. You didn't need to know a great deal about human beings to realize that the headmaster wasn't at all pleased with Bertrand.

'Well, Buckle?' he demanded, his eyebrows knitted together in a fierce frown. 'What have you got to say for yourself?'

'Nothing, sir. I'm very sorry, sir.'

This was what Bertrand always said to angry headmasters, even when he didn't really know why they were angry. Experience had taught him that this was the safest thing to do.

'I'm not surprised, Buckle. There's no possible excuse for your behaviour on Saturday. No excuse at all. What you did with those poor boys' clothes wasn't funny. It was nasty.'

'I didn't take them, sir.'

Now that Bertrand knew why he was in trouble, it was his turn to be upset. Surely he couldn't be held responsible for what ghosts did.

'Telling lies will only make it worse,' Mr Beak said sternly. 'Miss Bun saw you at the scene of the crime and so did the boys.'

'But . . .'

'There are no "buts", Buckle. You're not going to try to tell me that you had nothing to do with what happened, are you?'

'No, sir.'

Whatever his other faults, Bertrand was quite an honest boy.

'That's just as well. As you probably know, I don't like to resort to corporal punishment and what I'm about to do will hurt me far more than it will you but . . .'

Mr Beak droned on and on and Bertrand stopped listening. Unless George could do something to save him, he was going to be caned and that was that. After another couple of minutes, the headmaster instructed him to bend over the back of a chair and Bertrand did as he was told. It wasn't a new position for him but he still didn't enjoy it.

'Ghost,' he whispered out of the corner of his mouth. 'You'd better do something quick.'

'What did you say to me, Buckle.'

The headmaster had already selected a cane and was advancing on Bertrand.

'Nothing, sir.'

Although George had heard the whispered instruction, he wasn't quite sure what he could do. As George watched helplessly, the headmaster positioned himself beside Bertrand, balanced himself carefully and raised the cane high in the air.

'Ghost,' Bertrand whispered desperately. 'Remember the booby hatch.'

Unfortunately, Mr Beak heard the end part.

'What did you say about putting me in the booby hatch?' he demanded fiercely.

'Nothing, sir.'

'Oh yes you did. I'll soon teach you to be rude to me, you ill-mannered child. You're going to get six of the very best and you can keep count for me.'

The cane went up in the air again and George floated forward because he knew he couldn't afford to ignore Bertrand's warning. However much Bertrand might deserve to be punished, Mr Merryfellow was far more important.

As Mr Beak started to bring the cane down, George grabbed hold of it. He wasn't strong enough to prevent the cane from moving at all but instead of descending with a mighty thwack, it came down in slow motion and Bertrand received no more than a gentle tap. Mr Beak simply couldn't believe it and for a moment he thought the muscles in his shoulder had stopped working.

However, when he tried swishing the cane in the air, it moved easily enough. He wasn't to know that George had released it again.

'One, sir,' Bertrand said, grinning to himself.

'No, Buckle,' Mr Beak said firmly. 'That doesn't count. I was just practising.'

There was going to be no mistake this time. The headmaster rose up on his toes before bringing the cane down with all his strength. And once again George grabbed hold of it. The cane barely brushed against the seat of Bertrand's trousers.

'Is that one, sir?' Bertrand inquired.

'No, it isn't,' Mr Beak barked. 'Just keep quiet and leave the counting to me.'

When he tested, there still wasn't anything wrong with his shoulder so Mr Beak decided it must be the cane. He went over to his cane rack and selected another one. It swished most satisfactorily as he waved it through the air.

'Right, Buckle,' he said. 'Sorry to have kept you waiting.'

'That's all right, sir.'

But it wasn't all right. For the third time Mr Beak failed to give Bertrand more than a gentle tap. He was finding the experience most frustrating and George wasn't enjoying it much either. He was fed up with being waved backwards and forwards through the air at the end of a stick.

'Stop it for goodness sake, you silly old fool,' he

muttered, not realizing that he was speaking aloud.

'What did you say, Buckle?' Mr Beak demanded angrily.

'Nothing, sir.'

'Oh yes you did. I distinctly heard you call me a silly old fool.'

'I wouldn't do that, sir.'

Silly old fool, Bertrand thought to himself. He was sure that having a pet ghost must be the best thing that had ever happened to him.

'But I heard you, Buckle.'

'It was me,' George said.

Now he had started talking, George thought he might as well continue. Mr Beak was staring at the end of his cane in disbelief. There was nobody there but he was certain that this was where the voice had come from.

'Are you a ventriloquist, Buckle?'

'A ventrilowhat, sir?'

'Of course he isn't,' George said.

'You just did it again, Buckle.'

'Did what, sir?'

'Made the cane talk.'

'How would I do that, sir? I didn't hear the cane say anything.'

'Really? How strange.'

The talking cane was beginning to make Mr Beak a bit nervous and he examined it suspiciously. It looked normal enough and when he swished it through the air, it moved easily. Mr Beak decided that his imagination must be playing tricks. After all, he had been working very hard recently.

'Are you going to finish caning me, sir?' Bertrand asked politely.

'Of course I am, Buckle.'

'Oh no you're not,' George told him.

'Eeekkk,' shrieked Mr Beak. 'The cane just spoke to me again.'

Really frightened now, the headmaster tried to throw the cane away from him but instead of falling to the floor, it remained floating in mid-air because George was still holding on to it. Mr Beak wasn't to know this and he felt rather the same way Toby Tattle had with his clothes. He thought the cane must have come to life.

'Look at it now, Buckle,' Mr Beak screeched. 'I've got a talking cane that can fly.'

'Perhaps you can sell it to a circus, sir.'

Bertrand had remained bending over the chair.

'Look at it, I said.' Mr Beak was almost hysterical. 'It's flying round the office.'

It was all too much for Mr Beak and he covered his eyes with his hands to shut out the sight. Bertrand, smiling broadly all over his face, started to stand up and George let go of the cane. He was already ashamed about upsetting the headmaster so much. By the time Bertrand had turned round, the cane was laying harmlessly on the carpet.

'It's not flying now, sir.'

'Are you sure?'

Mr Beak kept his hands over his eyes.

'Yes, sir. The cane is on the carpet. It looks perfectly normal to me.'

'It's trying to trick us.' Mr Beak risked a quick peep between his fingers. 'It really was flying and talking, you know. I wasn't imagining things. I'm not mad.'

'Of course you aren't, sir.'

Bertrand's grin was broader than ever and Mr Beak noticed. However frightened he might be, he wasn't going to allow a child to laugh at him, especially if that child was Bertrand Buckle.

'Stop smirking and pick it up, Buckle,' he ordered. 'You'll soon see whether I'm telling the truth or not.'

'All right, sir.'

Bertrand did as he was told and picked up the cane. Although he had seen lots of canes, this was the first occasion Bertrand had actually held one in his hand. It felt good, very good indeed. He swished it through the air and the cane made a nice, whistling sound.

'Are you sure you weren't mistaken, sir? There doesn't seem to be anything wrong with it.'

'There wasn't when I tested it.' Mr Beak didn't know whether to be disappointed or relieved. 'The cane only came to life when I tried to use it.'

'What do you mean, sir?'

'When I tried to cane you, it wouldn't work. I could only give you a tap.'

'Perhaps there's something wrong with your arm, sir.'

'Of course there isn't anything wrong with my arm, you silly boy,' Mr Beak shouted. 'It's this confounded cane. Look, I'll bend over the chair while you try to whack me. You'll see then.'

Mr Beak was so upset by now that he was no longer thinking straight. As he watched the headmaster pull up his jacket and bend over the back of the chair, Bertrand could hardly believe his luck.

'Do you really want me to whack you, sir?'

'It's perfectly all right, Buckle. You won't hurt me. You can try to hit me as hard as you like.'

Bertrand didn't need to be told again. Gripping the cane firmly in both hands, he raised it high in the air before bringing it down with all his strength.

THWACK went the cane on Mr Beak's bottom.

'OOOWWW!' went the headmaster.

'I must be doing it wrong, sir,' Bertrand said quickly. 'I'd better try again.'

'Don't you d—,' Mr Beak began – but he was too late.

THWACK went the cane again.

'OOOWWW!' went Mr Beak.

'Thank you, ghost,' whispered Bertrand.

It was one of the happiest moments of his entire life. There were lots of boys who had been caned but Bertrand knew he must be the only boy in the world who had actually caned a headmaster.

Eight

By Monday afternoon, Mr Merryfellow was seriously concerned. He had hardly seen his friend at all over the weekend and now George was out again. After Bertrand had left for school that morning, Mr Merryfellow had gone all over the house shouting out George's name but there had been no reply. He had enjoyed no more success in the garden and, for the life of him, Mr Merryfellow had been unable to think where his friend might be. Ever since George had moved into the house, the two of them had spent their days together. It just wasn't like George to go off somewhere without telling Mr Merryfellow first.

It wasn't until Bertrand had returned from school and was out in the garden playing that George finally put in an appearance. The little ghost drifted into the kitchen while Mr Merryfellow was buttering some scones for tea and he immediately stopped what he was doing.

'Thank goodness, George,' he said, sighing

with relief. 'I've been worrying about you all day. I was beginning to think you might have been killed or something.'

George didn't even smile at the joke. Although it was difficult to tell with ghosts, Mr Merryfellow didn't think that his friend looked very well.

'Are you all right?' he inquired.

'I'm fine, thank you.'

Now Mr Merryfellow was convinced that something was wrong. George was normally such a cheerful little fellow but when he answered, he sounded as though he was ready to burst into tears.

'Where have you been all day?' Mr Merryfellow continued brightly, pretending he hadn't noticed.

'Out and about.'

'Did you go anywhere nice?'

'Not really.'

Mr Merryfellow was becoming more worried by the moment. He didn't know anything about ghost illnesses, or even if ghosts could be ill, but he was sure that George must be sickening for something. He didn't sound himself at all. Then Mr Merryfellow heard Bertrand shouting to an imaginary horse out in the garden and another possible explanation occurred to him. It could be something to do with Bertrand.

'Is it my nephew who's upsetting you?'

'What do you mean?'

This time George sounded guilty. Mr Merry-fellow was certain that he was on the right track.

'Having him here has messed up all the things we usually do together,' Mr Merryfellow explained, watching his friend carefully. 'You have to stay hidden for most of the day and I don't have so much time to spend with you. I was wondering if you might be a little bit jealous. It would only be natural if you were.'

Although Mr Merryfellow waited for an answer, George simply hovered where he was without saying a word.

'There's no need to be jealous,' he went on. 'You're still my friend. I like you just as much as ever. You know that, don't you?'

'Yes.'

George's voice was very small.

'Besides, it won't be for much longer. Bertrand will be going home in a few weeks.'

'I know.'

The words were almost a wail. To Mr Merry-fellow's amazement, he could see that there were tears welling up in George's eyes but before he could say anything more, the ghost had floated out of the kitchen as fast as he could.

By now Mr Merryfellow was really concerned. He determined to have a good chat with his friend later that night, after Bertrand had gone to bed. Somehow or other he had to discover what was upsetting George so much and try to help him. This was what friends were for, after all.

There was no doubt about it. It had been one of the most miserable days of George's death. Until now he had been sure that nothing could possibly be worse than his first haunt. This was the night George had discovered that instead of frightening people, he simply made them laugh. One day at school with Bertrand had been enough to convince George he was wrong.

After Bertrand had returned to class, and Mr Beak had gone home to rest in bed, George had been kept busy. Some of the things he was asked to do weren't too bad. For example, he had really enjoyed the games lesson. The boys had been playing football and Bertrand had told George to help him. Normally Bertrand wasn't a very good footballer but with George to assist him nobody else had had a chance. His side had won 27–0 and Bertrand scored all the goals. George had had just as much fun as Bertrand, keeping the ball away from the other boys. This, however, had been the exception: most of the things George had been forced to do were just plain nasty. Mr Russett could easily have hurt himself when he fell over after George had tied his shoelaces together and Miss Bun was definitely hurt by the drawing pin on her chair. Although the entire class had laughed when she jumped high in the air, George had known he shouldn't have done it. Jokes weren't a joke when somebody was hurt.

Nevertheless, George's depression hadn't been caused by what had happened at school. It was what Bertrand had told him on the way home which had made him so miserable.

'It was terrific,' Bertrand said enthusiastically. 'I've never enjoyed myself so much at school before. It was even better than when old Whacky accidentally stapled his tie to the desk and nearly strangled himself when he stood up.'

Although George hadn't answered, this didn't bother Bertrand.

'Wasn't I good at football?' he went on. 'Just think of it. I scored twenty-seven goals. That's more than I scored in my life before. With you to help me, they'll have to put me in the St Joseph's School team next year. I might even be captain.'

'I shan't be there to help you.'

'What do you mean?'

For a moment Bertrand didn't understand.

'When you go back to St Joseph's, I won't be with you,' George explained. 'I'll be here with your uncle.'

'That's right.' Bertrand was grinning. 'I haven't told you the good news yet, have I? I was saving it as a surprise.'

'A surprise?'

There was a sinking feeling in George's stomach. This was something which had been happening quite a lot since Bertrand had been around.

'You'll be coming back to London with me, ghost,' Bertrand said. 'You're going to stay with me for ever.'

'I can't do that.'

The very idea appalled George.

'Oh yes you can, ghost. If that's what I want, that's exactly what you're going to do.'

'I won't. My home is here. I'm not leaving Matthew.'

'Suit yourself.' Bertrand shrugged his shoulders as though he didn't care. 'You stay if that's what you want. I hope you'll both be very happy together in the booby hatch.'

No more was said but George had known that Bertrand was right. There was no way he could get out of it. Unless he wanted Matthew to suffer, he would have to go to London with Bertrand.

The conversation with Mr Merryfellow in the kitchen had only upset George more. It was impossible to tell his friend what was wrong and George knew he would be asked about it again as soon as Bertrand was in bed. George simply couldn't face it. It was unthinkable to lie to Mr Merryfellow yet it was equally impossible to tell him the truth. The only solution to the problem was to stay out of his friend's way. Then there wouldn't be any awkward questions to answer. Miserably, George had drifted off to the one place where he knew he would be left in peace. In

Fenella's empty crypt he hoped against hope that he would be able to think of some way to escape from Bertrand.

It was very quiet and peaceful, although the crypt seemed quite empty without Fenella's coffin. George stayed there until long after Mr Merry-fellow would have gone to bed, turning the problem over and over in his mind. However often he did so, the conclusion remained the same. He was trapped. There was nothing he could do.

Trying to convince himself that Bertrand wouldn't really do anything to harm his uncle was no good at all. By now George knew the boy well enough to realize that Bertrand was capable of anything. If George refused to go to London with him, Bertrand would tell everybody about Matthew living with a ghost. And if that happened, Matthew was likely to end up in the booby hatch he was so afraid of.

Even though he knew this, George didn't think he would be able to stand living with Bertrand, doing his bidding all the time. He had only been Bertrand's slave for three days now and it already seemed like an eternity. All the fun had gone out of George's death. He spent most of his time wondering what Bertrand would ask him to do next. The thought of having to do this for years, not days, made the little ghost shudder.

'I couldn't bear it,' he said out loud, two large tears trickling down his cheeks. 'I know I couldn't.'

'What couldn't you bear, Horrible?' a familiar voice asked from behind him.

George spun around, all thoughts of Bertrand temporarily forgotten. His tears dried unheeded on his cheeks.

'Fenella!' he exclaimed. 'What are you doing here?'

'I live here, remember.'

'But you're supposed to be in Transylvania.'

'I didn't like it,' Fenella explained, smiling at George's surprise and pleasure. 'Hardly anyone spoke in a language I could understand and Uncle Dracula was boring me back to life. All he could talk about was the good old nights. They sounded absolutely dreadful to me. Fancy having to bite all those dirty human necks. I couldn't stand it any longer so I decided to come home.'

Although Fenella chattered away cheerfully while the two of them helped the hearse driver to bring her things into the crypt, she hadn't forgotten what George had been saying when she came in. Or the tears she had seen glistening in his eyes. Once they both had a nice glass of hemlock wine in their hands and she was reclining gracefully in her coffin, Fenella reminded him about it.

'Why were you crying, Horrible?' she asked.

'It was nothing. I was just feeling a bit miserable.'

Even to his own ears, George didn't sound very convincing.

'There's more to it than that. Why, you don't look at all well. You're as pale as a human being. What is it that you can't bear?'

'I'm all right, really.' There seemed to be a lump in George's throat. When he went to London, he wouldn't see Fenella again either. 'There's no need for you to worry.'

'Oh yes there is,' Fenella said severely. 'I'm your friend, Horrible. If you can't talk to me, you can't talk to anybody.'

'That's just it, Fenella.' Despite himself, George could feel the tears welling up into his eyes again. 'I can't tell anybody. I promised not to.'

'Whom did you promise?'

'I promised Bertrand,' George sniffed.

'Bertrand?' Fenella had never heard of him. 'Who's he when he's at home?'

She was thinking that she had never seen George so upset. It was obvious to her that something truly terrible must have happened while she had been away.

'It was Bertrand Buckle,' George told her. 'He's Mr Merryfellow's nephew and he's come to stay.'

'I see.'

Fenella didn't see at all but now George had

started talking she didn't want him to stop. She took a sip of hemlock wine while she thought. If George was in trouble, and he obviously was, it was up to her to help him.

'This Bertrand Buckle,' she said. 'Has he done something nasty to you?'

'Something very nasty.' George spoke with great feeling.

'And he's made you promise not to tell anybody?'

'Yes.'

'Well, that's all right then. I'm not anybody, Horrible. I'm a vampire. Bertrand meant humans.'

'I don't know.' Although George desperately wanted Fenella to be right, he wasn't sure. A promise was very important to ghosts. It was unthinkable to break one. 'Even if you are a vampire, Fenella, you're still a body. You're in human shape.'

'All right, Horrible.' Fenella understood George's problem perfectly because promises were important to vampires too. It was only human beings who broke them. 'Would it be breaking your promise to tell the secret to a bat? Surely you didn't promise not to tell animals.'

'No, I didn't.' Suddenly there was a smile on George's face. 'It would be all right to tell a bat.'

'That's exactly what I thought,' Fenella said, smiling back. 'Just wait a minute.'

It only took a second for Fenella to change into her bat form and a second more to fly up to the roof of the crypt where she hung upside down. As soon as she was comfortable, George began to tell her what had been happening while she was away. He didn't miss out anything and the longer he went on, the more horrified Fenella became. She might never have seen Bertrand but she didn't need to in order to realize what a little beast he must be. When George reached the part where Bertrand had told him he would have to go back to London with him, Fenella gasped out loud.

'That's monstrous,' she exclaimed. 'It's the nastiest thing I've heard in my entire death.'

'I know.' Although it had been a relief to explain his problems to someone, it still made George miserable to think about what he would have to do.

'There just isn't a way out, though. Unless I do as Bertrand says, poor Matthew will suffer. I can't allow that.'

'That's where you're wrong, George Horrible Ghastly.' Fenella was fluttering her wings with excitement. 'There might not be anything you can do on your own but there's an awful lot we can do together, especially if you ask your family to help.'

As Fenella started to explain her plan to him, George began to cheer up. By the time she had finished, he was smiling all over his face. It would

106

work, George just knew it would. When they had finished with Bertrand, he would wish he had never even heard of ghosts.

Nine

By the following night Mr Merryfellow was really worried about George. He even thought of contacting the police until he realized how ridiculous that would be. He could just imagine what PC Snatchem would say if he telephoned to report a missing ghost.

All the same, Mr Merryfellow was most concerned. He hadn't seen hide nor hair of his friend since their conversation in the kitchen. On the Monday night he not only went through every room in the house but checked the freezer and fridge as well. At first, Mr Merryfellow thought George might be playing a game of hide-and-seek. When the ghost hadn't appeared by bedtime, he began to fear the worst.

'Something bad has happened to George,' Mr Merryfellow said to himself. 'I knew there was something wrong when I saw him in the kitchen.'

He was even more convinced of this after George didn't appear the next morning. The trouble was, there was absolutely nothing Mr Merryfellow could do. He couldn't go to the police and there was nobody else he could ask. He might have had a better idea of what to do if he had had any inkling as to what George's problem was. It had to be more than simple jealousy of Bertrand but for the life of him Mr Merryfellow couldn't think what. George seemed to have completely disappeared and Mr Merryfellow was a very troubled man when he went to bed on the Tuesday.

However, Mr Merryfellow wasn't the only troubled person in the house. His nephew was upset as well. Bertrand had had a lot of plans for the Tuesday but when George didn't appear, he had to go to school on his own. This made him absolutely furious.

'That sneaky little ghost has done a runner,' he muttered angrily. 'It's not fair, not when I've been so good to him. I'll show him what's what when he does come back.'

But George didn't come back and Bertrand returned home from school determined to do something. Like his uncle, though, he wasn't exactly sure what he could do. After he had gone to bed that night, he made one final attempt to get in touch with George.

'Ghost,' he said, addressing the empty bedroom. 'I know you're there so you'd better come out.'

There was no reply. No ghost appeared at his bidding.

'I'm going to count to ten,' Bertrand continued. 'If you haven't shown yourself by then, Uncle Matthew can book his ticket to the booby hatch.'

Bertrand slowly counted to ten. When he had finished, he was still all alone in the bedroom. His tame ghost obviously wasn't as tame as he had thought.

'That does it, ghost,' he announced. 'Unless I see you by the morning, poor old Uncle Matthew is for the high jump.'

George, who was hovering invisibly in a corner of the bedroom, couldn't understand why his friend would be doing any jumping in the morning but this did nothing to stop his broad, satisfied smile. Bertrand would be seeing him before morning all right, and a lot, lot more besides.

For some reason Bertrand couldn't get to sleep. No matter how he tossed and turned, he couldn't get himself comfortable. Although it had been a warm day, the bedroom was distinctly chilly and there were a lot of little creakings and tappings that he hadn't noticed on other nights. Bertrand didn't scare easily but he was gradually becoming nervous. He began to imagine that there were hideous monsters lurking in the darkness, just waiting to pounce on him.

'Bertrand.'

The voice from close beside his bed made him jump.

'Is that you, ghost?' After the initial fright, Bertrand had recognized George's voice. 'I thought you'd come back.'

'I want to tell you something,' George continued as though Bertrand hadn't spoken. 'You're a nasty, mean little boy and I refuse to do anything more for you.'

'Oh yeah.' Bertrand was getting his confidence back by now. 'What about Uncle Matthew?'

'You're going to make me a promise.' Once again it was as though George hadn't heard Bertrand. 'From now on you're to promise to be well behaved and not to do anything naughty.'

This time Bertrand laughed out loud.

'You're talking a load of codswallop, ghost. You sound as though you should be in the booby hatch yourself. You're off your rocker.'

'If you don't promise,' George continued, 'it will be the worse for you. You'll have to be punished.'

'Who's going to do that?' Bertrand sneered. 'You and whose army? You don't scare me, ghost.'

'Will you promise?' George asked.

'Of course I won't, stupid. All I promise is that I'll do just as I like and you'll help me.'

'In that case, Bertrand Buckle, I've done all I can. You have been warned.'

Although Bertrand called out to him several times, there was no reply from George. Either he had gone away or he was refusing to answer.

'Silly ghost,' Bertrand said. 'He should know by now that he can't frighten me. Just wait till the morning. I'll soon show him who's the boss.'

Bertrand settled down again but sleep still didn't come easily. The bedroom seemed colder than ever and the creaks and tappings were even louder. He tried counting sheep but this didn't help. Bertrand ran out of fingers and toes too quickly.

He was still wide awake when the church clock began to strike midnight. As he lay in his bed and listened, Bertrand noticed that there was a strange smell in the bedroom. At first he assumed it must be him.

'I'd better have a bath tomorrow,' he thought. 'My feet don't half pong.'

But it wasn't his feet. The smell grew worse and worse until Bertrand could hardly breathe. It was like having a thousand stink bombs all set off together. It was the odour of dirty drains, smelly socks, rotting rubbish, bad breath and acrid armpits all combined in one monstrous smell which was almost unbearable.

'I'm getting out of here,' Bertrand gasped, throwing back the covers.

'Wait,' a ghostly voice commanded.

The one word was enough to have Bertrand back under the covers in a flash. This was no ghost like George. This was a real ghost, a ghost who smelled as though she had just come from the grave and had a voice like the creak of a coffin lid being opened. Bertrand was terrified and he could feel all the hairs on his head standing up on end. This was what happened to most humans who met George's mother. Mrs Ghastly had been haunting for more years than she cared to remember and she was very good at her work.

'That should teach the little whippersnapper to mess around with my Horrible,' she said in a voice no human ear could detect. 'Come on, husband, it's your turn now. Do your stuff and don't forget your lines.'

'Why would I forget my lines?' Mr Ghastly demanded angrily. 'I've done more haunts than you've had cobweb sandwiches.'

'You forget where you've left your head often enough. I seem to spend half my death finding it for you.'

'Mum, Dad,' George interrupted before the argument could progress any further. 'This isn't the time to argue.'

'You're right, son,' Mr Ghastly agreed. 'Just leave it to me. I'll teach that brat a lesson he won't forget in a hurry.'

While the Ghastly family had been talking

among themselves, Bertrand had been huddled under the bedclothes. At first he had been shaking with fear but gradually he calmed down. The terrible smell seemed to have gone and he was beginning to think he must have been mistaken about the voice. Nothing else seemed to have happened.

Cautiously he poked his head out from under the covers. The smell was definitely going. Although there was still a faint, musty odour in the bedroom, it was nothing like it had been before. When he looked around, there were no ghosts to be seen.

'I must have been imagining things,' Bertrand said. 'It was all a figtree of my imagination. There wasn't really a voice at all.'

'Oh yes there was, Bertrand Buckle.'

This second voice was far, far more terrifying than the first and for a few seconds Bertrand was paralysed with fear. He wanted to duck down under the covers again but he seemed unable to move. As he lay there, staring wide-eyed into the darkness, something started to materialize beside his bed, something so hideous that Bertrand could hardly believe his eyes. It was a head, a wrinkled, balding head which seemed to glow slightly in the darkness, giving the deep-set eyes a mad glint. It was a face straight out of a nightmare – but it wasn't this which frightened Bertrand so much. What was really awful was that the head was floating there on its own, without any sign of the body it should have belonged to.

'Aren't you going to say hello?' the head asked, grinning evilly and showing a mouthful of yellow teeth.

Bertrand most certainly wasn't. Suddenly he could move again and he ducked under the blankets like a ferret going down a rabbit hole. Huddled there, quaking with fear, Bertrand began to suspect that messing around with ghosts wasn't such a good idea after all. A moment later he knew he was right because the terrifying head was there under the blankets with him, still grinning evilly.

'Get away from me,' Bertrand shrieked.

As he spoke, he struck out at the apparition with his fist but there was nothing solid for him to hit. His hand seemed to go right through the head.

'That wasn't very friendly,' it said. 'Anybody would think you weren't pleased to see me.'

'Wh-wh-what do you w-w-want?' Bertrand asked, his voice trembling.

The words seemed to stick in his mouth. He would have liked to run away but he seemed hypnotized by the hideous eyes: he just couldn't tear his own eyes away from them.

'J-j-just a pr-pr-promise,' the head mimicked unkindly. 'Promise to behave yourself and leave my son alone.'

It was on the tip of Bertrand's tongue to shout out that he promised but something stopped him. Frightened as he was, he didn't want to give up his own ghost.

'Wh-wh-what w-w-will you d-d-do if I d-d-don't?'

'In that case we'll be seeing quite a lot of each other,' Mr Ghastly promised. 'If you don't agree to leave George alone, I shan't leave you alone either. I shall come visiting every night. You don't want that, do you?'

'N-n-no.'

Bertrand most certainly didn't. On the other hand, he was feeling braver by the minute. However horrible the head might be, he was remembering something George had told him while they had been talking about ghosts. When he spoke again, Bertrand had lost his stutter.

'You can't do anything else if I don't promise, though,' he said. 'Ghosts can haunt human beings but they can't hurt them, can they?'

Mr Ghastly's grin became even wider and for a terrible moment Bertrand thought George must have been wrong. The head's next words came as a distinct relief.

'That's true,' Mr Ghastly admitted. 'I can't do anything to hurt you.'

'Well, I shan't promise then. Bring your rotten old head here every night and see if I care. However ugly you are, I'll soon get used to you.'

117

'You're making a bad mistake, Bertrand Buckle,' Mr Ghastly warned him.

'It's you that's made the mistake, turnip-head.' Bertrand was feeling really confident by now. 'I'm not a soppy little girl. I don't scare so easily. I've got my own ghost and I'm going to keep him, so you can jolly well clear off and leave me to get some sleep.'

'You don't understand, you beastly little child.' Mr Ghastly's smile had vanished. 'I may not be able to do anything to harm you but I have friends who are far worse than I am. If you want to see what I mean, just put your head out from under the blankets.'

Before Bertrand had a chance to ask Mr Ghastly what he meant, the head had gone. For a minute or two, Bertrand stayed where he was, thinking about what the head had told him. It didn't take him long to decide that the head had been lying.

'It was bluffing,' he said to himself. 'There's nothing out there. In any case, ghosts can't hurt me.'

Without giving himself an opportunity to change his mind, Bertrand popped his head out from beneath the covers. The first thing he saw was Fenella who had been waiting patiently beside the bed. It was as though a great, icy hand had seized hold of Bertrand's heart. Even breathing was difficult. When he opened

118

his mouth to scream, not even a squeak came out.

'Do you know what I am, Bertrand?'

Fenella's voice was almost a hiss. Bertrand's was nonexistent. There was still no sound when he tried to speak, so he had to nod his head. He had never been so frightened in all his life.

'Do you know what I can do to you, Bertrand?'

Another nod of the head. It was like a nightmare and Bertrand would have liked to pinch himself to find out if he was really awake. Unfortunately, he was so terrified he seemed unable to move anything apart from his head. It was as though he was mesmerized.

'Do you want me to get angry with you, Bertrand?'

Bertrand shook his head so hard that it was in danger of falling off. He knew all about vampires from the comics he read. Only none of the monsters in the comics gave any idea of how hideous a real vampire was.

'In that case, I'd better explain something to you, Bertrand,' Fenella's voice was more of a hiss than ever. 'George is a friend of mine. A very good friend and when he's upset, I'm upset too. I'm sure you don't want that, do you?'

Bertrand had never wanted anything less in his life and he was shaking his head so hard it was almost a blur. He didn't even want a vampire as a friend. He just wanted Fenella to go away and leave him in peace.

'I didn't think you would.' Fenella's smile made her look even more awful, especially as she had leaned forward slightly. The mere sight of her teeth gave Bertrand goose pimples all over. 'It might be sensible if you make the promise George asked for.'

As if by magic, Bertrand recovered his voice.

'I promise, I promise,' he screeched. 'I'll do anything you want.'

'I thought you might,' Fenella said. 'George, Bertrand is ready to talk to you now.'

'Thank you, Fenella.' In response to Fenella's call, George had appeared at her side. 'I can handle Bertrand now. Don't go too far away, though.'

'I won't, Horrible,' Fenella promised fondly. 'Just call if you need me.'

Then, to Bertrand's relief, she was gone. However, George remained and he was looking very stern.

'There's going to be a big change in our relationship from now on,' he told Bertrand. 'Unless you want to tangle with Fenella and the rest of my family again, you're going to do exactly as I say. Is that clearly understood?'

'Oh yes, ghost.' Bertrand was almost babbling. 'Please don't call that horrible, hideous vampire back again. Just tell me what you want me to do.'

George started to explain, feeling very pleased with himself. By the time he had finished with Bertrand, Mr Merryfellow would have a nephew he could be really proud of.

Ten

'Are you sure you have everything, Bertrand?' Mr Merryfellow asked.

'Yes thank you, Uncle. I checked again after I'd tidied up my bedroom.'

Bertrand was also looking very tidy himself as he stood on Gigglesworth Station, the door to his carriage open. His skin was pink instead of grey, his teeth white not yellow. What was more, his hair was neatly brushed and there wasn't a single hole in his clothes. Mr Whackem and his parents would have had the greatest difficulty in recognizing the scruffy boy who had left London a month earlier.

'I shall miss you when you've gone, you know,' Mr Merryfellow went on.

'I shall miss you too, Uncle Matthew. It's been a really wonderful holiday. The moment I get home I shall write you a proper thank-you letter.'

'There's no need, Bertrand.'

'I want to, Uncle.'

Just then Bertrand spotted an elderly lady coming along the platform, struggling with a heavy suitcase. He rushed towards her immediately.

'Let me carry that for you,' he said.

He carried the suitcase to her compartment and heaved it up on to the luggage rack for her. Only when she was comfortably settled did he return to his uncle.

'You're such a thoughtful boy, Bertrand,' Mr Merryfellow said admiringly. 'You'd better be getting aboard yourself now. The train will be leaving in a moment.'

'All right, Uncle. Can I give you this first, though?'

Bertrand pulled a neatly wrapped package from his pocket and gave it to Mr Merryfellow.

'What is it?'

'It's just a little present I bought for you.'

'A present? How nice, but you really shouldn't have wasted your money on an old fogey like me.'

'It was the least I could do to repay you for your kindness.'

Mr Merryfellow would have opened the parcel straight away but the station master had blown his whistle and there was a last minute rush to get Bertrand aboard. George, who had been hovering invisibly nearby, went on the train with him. He had his own farewells to say but he waited until

the train had started to move before he revealed his presence.

'You're doing well, Bertrand,' he said approvingly.

'I know. I'm turning into a proper little goody-goody.'

Bertrand was no longer surprised when voices spoke to him out of thin air. George had been staying very close to him for the past few weeks.

'Make sure you keep it up,' George warned him. 'We'll be keeping check on you. Any backsliding and Fenella will be popping in to visit you one dark night.'

'Don't worry, ghost. I'll behave.'

'Goodbye then. I'd better be leaving.'

'Goodbye, ghost.'

George floated off and Bertrand settled back in his seat. He wasn't sorry to be left on his own. In the end, having a ghost around hadn't been nearly as much fun as he had imagined and the thought of a whole lifetime of being good made him feel quite ill. On the other hand, the very idea of meeting Fenella again brought him out in goose bumps. Not for the first time, Bertrand wondered whether the library was likely to have a book explaining how to tame a vampire. He would have to check as soon as he was back in London.

* * *

'I don't know whether to be pleased or sorry,' Mr Merryfellow said.

'What do you mean?' George asked.

Now the train had gone, the two of them were driving home. Although George was sitting in the front seat beside his friend, he had to remain invisible. He didn't want to startle the drivers of other cars.

'It's difficult to explain, George. I've enjoyed having Bertrand to stay and I'm sorry he's left. At the same time, I'm glad that I'll be able to spend more time with you again. It just hasn't been the same these last few weeks, has it? There have been whole days when I've hardly seen you.'

'I know.'

George was smiling to himself. His friend had no idea how different the last few weeks had been.

'It must have been far worse for you, George. I mean, you had to stay hidden nearly all the time.'

'It was difficult,' George agreed.

'Were you lonely?'

'Not really. I missed your company but there were plenty of other things to do.'

Like making sure that Bertrand behaved himself. Since the night in Bertrand's bedroom, George had spent most of his time keeping a careful eye on the boy.

'That Bertrand is a lovely child, though,' Mr

Merryfellow continued. 'I've never known such a helpful boy. Why, it's so long since I've had to do any washing-up that I've almost forgotten how to do it. And he kept his bedroom so tidy it made me feel quite ashamed of all the mess I leave lying around. It must be the way his parents brought him up.'

'He certainly must have been trained well.'

George was smirking to himself again. He knew exactly who it was who had done the training.

'Mind you, George, he wasn't like that at first. I didn't like to say anything to you but I was really worried about him. There was all that trouble at school, for example. There were even times when I thought he might be a nasty little boy. Then he changed overnight. Perhaps he just needed time to settle in.'

'Perhaps.'

There was no way George could tell his friend the truth. As far as Mr Merryfellow was concerned, Bertrand shouldn't even have known that there was a ghost in the house. George could hardly explain to him that for the last few weeks he had been telling Bertrand exactly how to behave.

'It was nice of Bertrand to buy me a present,' Mr Merryfellow went on. 'It's probably a box of chocolates.'

Mr Merryfellow was very partial to chocolates.

'Do you want me to open it for you?'

'That's a good idea.'

George started unwrapping the package. As ghost fingers weren't very good at fiddly jobs like this, it took him a minute or two. By the time he had finished, Mr Merryfellow was becoming quite excited. He had always loved to receive presents.

'What is it, George?' he demanded as soon as most of the paper had been removed.

'It's a book.'

'How nice.' Mr Merryfellow enjoyed reading as much as he enjoyed eating chocolates. 'What's it about?'

'Wait a minute.'

George pulled the rest of the paper away, then he started to laugh. He simply couldn't stop himself.

'It's a book of ghost stories,' he spluttered.

'A book of ghost stories?' Mr Merryfellow was puzzled. He couldn't understand why his nephew had bought him a book about ghosts or why George was laughing so much. 'I wonder why he chose that.'

'I wonder.'

George was laughing more than ever. The answer was a secret which Mr Merryfellow would never be able to share.